contents

SPECIAL FEATURES

Sunset

curtains, draperies & shades

By the Editors of
Sunset Books

Sunset Books ■ Menlo Park, California

SUNSET BOOKS

Vice President, General Manager: Richard A. Smeby
Vice President, Editorial Director: Bob Doyle
Production Director: Lory Day
Director of Operations: Rosann Sutherland
Art Director: Vasken Guiragossian

CURTAINS, DRAPERIES & SHADES was produced
in conjunction with Roundtable Press, Inc.
Directors: Marsha Melnick, Susan E. Meyer, Julie Merberg

STAFF FOR THIS BOOK:

Developmental Editor: Linda J. Selden
Editor: Linda Hetzer
Text: Linda Lee
Art Direction: Areta Buk/Thumb Print
Illustrations: Beverley Bozarth Colgan
Materials Photography: Tom Haynes
Photo Research: Toby Greenberg
Production Assistant: Sara Newberry

COVER: Double layers of soft Roman shades control light and
add softness to this inviting bay. Interior design by Tres McKinney.
Cover design by Vasken Guiragossian. Photography by E. Andrew
McKinney. Photo styling by JoAnn Masaoka Van Atta.

For additional copies of *Curtains, Draperies & Shades* or any
other Sunset book, call 1-800-526-5111.
Or see our website at: www.sunsetbooks.com

PHOTO CREDITS

Bruce hardwood floors: *30 top*
Rosemary Carroll: *9 (Judy Girod, Girodesign, NY)*
Phillip Ennis: *4–5 (Eliz Read Weber Designs); 27 top
    left (Butler's Of Far Hills/Jeffrey Haines); 31 (Norman
    Michaeloff); 33 bottom (Butler's Of Far Hills/Jeffrey
    Haines); 56 bottom (Aves, Inc./John Widdicomb ;
    85 (Barbara Ostrom Associates); 87 (Denise Balaser);
    103 bottom (Butler's Of Far Hills/Jeffrey Haines);
    108 top (Rug and Kilim); 111 top (Design
    Consultants/Gail Whiting)*
Everett&Soule: *12 right (Marc Michaels for Bamboo
    Homes); 86 bottom (Sisler Williams Interior Design,
    Jacksonville, FL); 89 bottom (Robb & Stucky, Altamonte
    Springs, FL); 113 top (Sisler Williams Interior Design,
    Jacksonville, FL)*
Tria Giovan: *6; 26 top right; 27 bottom right; 30 bottom;
    35 top; 66 top & bottom;69 top; 84; 108 bottom*
Jamie Hadley: *33 top*
Johnson Group/Kirsch: *32 top; 34*
Dennis Krukowski: *11; 12 left; 26 top left and center
    right (Donna Lang and Lucretia Robertson); 68 top
    (Judy Petersen)*
E. Andrew McKinney: *8 bottom; 13; 56 top; 67 top;
    88 top; 102; 103 top*
Melabee M Miller: *Title page (Lisa Melone, Summit, NJ);
    68 bottom (Suzanne Curtis, ASID, Ho-Ho Kus, NJ);
    109 (Marilee Schemp, ASID, Summit, NJ)*
Bradley Olman: *8 top (Ms. Scott); 27 top right
    (Terry Ervin)*
Robert Perron: *110 top (Ann Sargent, Designer,
    E. Thetford, VT)*
Kenneth Rice Photography/www.kenricephoto.com:
    26 bottom left; 57 bottom
Mark Samu: *copyright page; 10 top & bottom (Courtesy
    Hearst Publications); 32 bottom (Doug Moyer Architect);
    86 top (The Tile Studio); 111 bottom (Beverly Balk
    Design)*
Michael Skott: *113 bottom*
Smith + Noble Windoware (1 800 765-7776/
    www.smithandnoble.com): *7 top and bottom; 26 bottom
    right; 28–29; 35 bottom; 57 top; 64; 65 top and bottom;
    67 bottom; 69 bottom*
Jessie Walker: *26 center left (Star Norini-Johnson, CKD,
    ASID Distinctive Kitchen Designs, Inc. Wauconda, IL);
    27 bottom left (Truffles, Kim Elia Designer, Naperville,
    IL); 88 bottom (Gabrielle Rousso Designs, Highland
    Park, IL) ; 89 top (Truffles, Dianne Lynn Designer,
    Naperville, IL); 110 bottom; 112 top & bottom*

getting started

b uying fabric and sewing the project may be
the most pleasurable part of making a window
treatment, but the planning process is where the real
work is done. It's the key to a successful project.

Knowing what your options are for various styles
of windows and understanding the basics of how
color, pattern, and texture affect the overall look
can make a real difference in the final product.
Take time to find the style that's right for you, look
at fabric samples in your home at different times of
the day, and think about your lifestyle and
preferences before you begin.

a look at window treatments

If you're tired of staring at a bare or poorly dressed window, it's hard to resist the urge to buy some fabric, set up the machine, and start sewing. But, like any project, a successful window treatment relies on some thoughtful decision making.

First, become familiar with the various styles and terms so you'll know how to tell a curtain from a drapery and a valance from a cornice. Then, let an awareness of your functional and decorative needs, as well as your personal style, guide you in choosing the treatment that's right for you.

coming to terms

If you haven't kept up with window treatment fashions, you're in for a pleasant surprise. Familiar styles have been joined by a collection of innovative top treatments, from casual valances to classic swags and cascades. Here's a brief look at your options.

CURTAINS. By definition, curtains are gathered on a rod or attached to a rod by tabs, ties, or rings. If the curtains open and close, it's by hand.

In general, length sets the style with curtains. Café curtains cover only the lower half of the window, ending at the sill or apron. With cafés, use a generous amount of fabric so they don't look skimpy.

Full-length curtains lend themselves to both elegant and informal schemes. Curtains that are tied in poufs called bishop's sleeves and curtains that puddle on the floor impart a luxurious mood; in contrast, simple floor-length curtains tied back above the sash create a casual effect.

Curtains combine well with other treatments. If you like the look of stationary curtain panels but you want some privacy, pair the curtains with miniblinds or a pleated shade. For a more finished effect, top them with a cornice or valance.

DRAPERIES. Long considered staid and predictable, today's draperies offer a variety of intriguing pleat styles and decorative hardware.

Draperies have pleated headings that attach to rods by means of drapery hooks. They are opened and closed either by hand or by a traverse rod system.

Pinch pleats, the traditional drapery heading, consist of three shallow folds tacked at the base. Variations of this

LEFT: **Simple curtain panels, hung by rings from a slim rod, are among the most versatile window treatment styles. Here, the leading edge of each panel is turned back to reveal a plaid lining.**

basic style include goblet, reverse pinch, and butterfly. Other styles such as pencil pleats are achieved with the use of pleating tapes sewn to the back of the drapery heading.

Though most draperies that are hung on conventional or decorative rods are meant to be opened and closed, drapery panels can also be stationary. Pleated side panels tie back beautifully because the pleats form consistent folds.

SHADES. Shades offer an enormous array of versatile and different-looking styles. Moreover, shades are as hardworking as they are good-looking, ensuring privacy, controlling light, and conserving energy.

Roman, balloon, and cloud shades all raise and lower by means of cords threaded through rings sewn to the back of the shade. From the front of a flat Roman shade, you see crisp, tailored folds. A variation, called a soft-fold Roman shade, has extra fabric in the folds to give the shade some body and shape even when it's lowered.

Pleats in balloon shades create billowy poufs at the lower edge. The shirring at the top of a cloud shade adds softness.

Because they're inexpensive and easy to make, roller shades are popular in informal areas and in children's rooms. Top them with a simple valance or cornice.

TOP: Pinch-pleated draperies operate easily on traverse rods. They retain their crisp look for the life of the drapery and are always in style.

BOTTOM: Shades such as this swagged Roman shade require less fabric than panels and keep the window simple. They are easy to operate and allow in light as they ensure privacy.

VALANCES. Some valances, such as rod-pocket, Roman, and balloon, look like short versions of their longer counterparts. Others are more innovative, sporting shaped, poufed, or rolled lower edges.

Used alone, valances bring a whisper of style and color to windows. Placed over another treatment, they not only conceal the heading but also lend a decorative flourish. Arched, tapered, or scalloped valances crown curtains and draperies, adding flowing lines and visual interest. Box-pleated valances provide a classic top treatment for tailored draperies. In children's rooms, a skirt or stagecoach valance can dress up a blind or roller shade.

The lower edges of valances offer unlimited possibilities for trimmings, from ruffles and piping to contrast banding and fringe.

CORNICES. Because their edges are so clearly delineated, cornices add architectural interest. The effect depends, in part, on the shape of the lower edge; straight cornices are simple and tailored; those with scallops are more formal.

When used on more than one window in a room, cornices unify the space and create a pleasing visual rhythm. They also display the fabric's design over a flat area.

In addition, cornices serve two very practical purposes: they cover the heading and hardware at the top of the undertreatment, and they block cold drafts coming from the window.

TOP: **A valance conceals the curtain heading and gives the top of the window a finished look. This straight valance in a bold allover print pulls together colors from various elements of the room furnishings.**

BOTTOM: **Upholstered cornices, gently scalloped and trimmed at the lower edge, add height to a pair of small windows. The roller shades underneath are handsome as well as practical.**

SWAGS AND CASCADES. Among the most impressive of all window treatments, swags and cascades bring distinction and classic form to windows. Once found in only the most opulent settings, today's versions can be more casual and adapt to informal decorating schemes as well.

Challenging to make and mount, traditional and cutout swags look like flowing lengths of fabric. Usually, they're accompanied by cascades. For a more formal look, put swags and cascades over long side panels or on top of sheers.

Easy-to-make running swags can be wrapped around a pole, draped in decorative swag holders, or held in place with knots or tabs.

RIGHT: Swags and cascades hung over luxurious drapery panels create a look of elegance. The black-and-white diagonal trim defines the fabric edges and emphasizes the soaring height of the windows.

THE ROLE OF A WINDOW

Windows are designed to admit light and air and allow in views of the outside world. But windows and their treatments play a myriad of other roles, ranging from functional to purely decorative.

LIGHT. *The primary function of windows is to provide natural light. How much light actually enters the room depends on your window treatment choice. To admit the maximum amount of light into the room, choose a treatment that stacks back completely. To filter light, choose sheers, laces, and casement fabrics. To block the light, select curtains, draperies, and shades lined with blackout linings.*

CLIMATE. *To take advantage of refreshing breezes, choose treatments that completely clear the window. Heavy fabrics block the flow of air more than lightweight ones. Most window treatments have an insulating effect, because they inhibit air from circulating.*

PRIVACY. *Any window in your home has the potential for allowing people to see inside. Sheers and lightweight fabrics let in some light during the day while providing privacy, but you'll need a heavier window covering that closes completely for total privacy.*

NOISE CONTROL. *Window treatments can reduce noise from both outside and inside the house. In general, the softer and more generous the treatment, the more sound it will absorb.*

VIEW. *When the view deserves to be seen, either choose a fabric that repeats the color and pattern on the wall so as not to distract the eye from the view beyond or choose a treatment that frames the window like a work of art. When the view is unattractive, select bold patterns and colors so that the window treatment itself attracts attention, or obscure the view with sheer or semisheer fabrics.*

color, pattern, and texture

A well-planned window treatment combines the basic design elements of color, pattern, and texture with subtle design concepts to create a beautiful, balanced effect.

color

No matter which window treatment you prefer, your first decisions will be about color. The following tips will help you choose and combine colors:

✂ To develop a color sense, look through decorating magazines and books and pull or mark examples of fabrics, window treatments, and rooms that appeal to you. Though they may seem unrelated at first, you'll gradually see a pattern to your preferences.

✂ Take your color cues from colors you and other members of the household love in nature, in fashion, and in interiors.

✂ If you want to create more visual space or a background for other interesting items in a room, choose a color for your window treatment that matches or is a similar value to the wall color. If you want to create interest and take your eye away from other elements in a room, choose a contrasting color from the wall color.

✂ Low value, less-intense colors may "wear" better visually than strong ones.

✂ Color changes with the lighting. Purchase a yard of the fabric that you are considering, tape it to the wall, and look at it throughout the day and by artificial light at night.

✂ The impact of color is intensified when it's used in large quantities. The color that you may have been considering for a full-length window treatment may be better used as an accent pillow or a simple valance or swag.

OPPOSITE TOP: **Lined curtains in a subtle floral print open and close handily on striking iron rods and rings. The allover pattern adds interest to the windows.**

OPPOSITE BOTTOM: **Using a vertical-stripe fabric on a swagged Roman shade adds an element of surprise as the pattern follows the gentle curved edges.**

ABOVE: **Bold stripes create tailored curtains and a pleated valance. A cord threaded through grommets in the heading adds a nautical note.**

✂Color is affected by the direction of light. Windows facing south and east let in warm, cheering light. Indirect northern light is softer and cooler, and light from the west is harshest of all.

pattern

Pattern enriches any decorating scheme, adding depth, movement, and visual interest. The following tips on using and combining pattern will help you gain pattern confidence.

✂Patterns that share at least one color combine easily.

✂The size of the pattern should correspond to the scale of the room and its windows. Small-scale patterns are often used in cozy rooms. Large-scale patterns create the impression that a room is smaller than it actually is, so may be better shown in spacious rooms.

✂Similar patterns of different scales also combine well, such as small checks and larger plaids.

✂Pattern combinations can be simple, such as the unpatterned walls, windows, and furnishings seen in the clean Shaker style as well as in more formal schemes. Another approach is to use pattern throughout—on the windows, on the walls, even on the furnishings. This all-out mix of patterns, reminiscent of Victorian times, is tricky to pull off. A more doable strategy is to combine pattern with plain color for a balanced look. Keeping walls plain while dressing windows in pattern draws attention to the window and the window treatment.

✂Consider how a pattern will appear placed on different surfaces. A full-length gathered or pleated window treatment will look entirely different from a flat Roman shade, even when the same fabric is used for both.

✂Avoid combining too many patterns in one area. A good rule of thumb is to use one bold pattern on a large surface so that it predominates. Then add two or possibly three smaller-scale patterns, distributing them around the room in order to avoid pattern clusters.

texture

Shimmering faille, nubby woven wool, and tasseled fringe—all window treatment materials possess texture, from distinctive to subtle.

When the texture is smooth, light is reflected and colors appear lighter and more lustrous, and often a bit formal.

When there's more texture, fabric appears duller because the light is absorbed rather than reflected. Notice-ably textured fabrics tend to be casual.

A monochromatic color scheme with very little pattern allows for more texture than a scheme with bold color and pattern. For a beautiful blend of rough and smooth surfaces throughout a room, try to introduce enough texture to create interest, but not so much that visual chaos results.

ABOVE LEFT: A padded valance and a soft cloud shade in a bright plaid stand out against another plaid of the same value and scale on the wall.

ABOVE RIGHT: Basic flat panels in a plaid fabric are striking when folded back to expose a print lining. The treatment becomes a grand backdrop for the bed.

OPPOSITE: A novelty sheer fabric for curtain panels creates interest as it helps to camouflage the view.

before you sew

Whether you're sewing a single shade or draping a wall of windows, you'll undoubtedly have to handle much more fabric than for most sewing projects. You'll need plenty of room and probably some special tools.

space to work

Staking out and organizing a special work area is worth the time it takes, even if it steals some living space for a while. A sewing room with a large table and special nooks and crannies for supplies is ideal. If you don't have the luxury of a sewing room and table, you'll need a large, flat surface on which to measure, cut, and sew.

As an alternative to a table, consider a piece of plywood or a hollow flush door. As a base for either one, you can use a pair of sawhorses or a table (protected with a blanket). If you choose sawhorses, you'll need rigid plywood $3/4$ to 1 inch thick. It's best to pad your work surface. For details, see page 15.

tools of the trade

The following list includes all the tools necessary for making window treatments, as well as some that are very useful though not essential.

MEASURING TOOLS

A spring-return 12-foot or longer *steel tape measure* assures easy, accurate measuring of windows. For measuring fabric, a 100-inch synthetic tape is convenient.

A *carpenter's square,* available at hardware stores, is essential for squaring off the ends of yardage. A 12-by-24-inch perfectly smooth square is better than a smaller one.

A 32-by 40-inch piece of *matte board* with the corners cut exactly

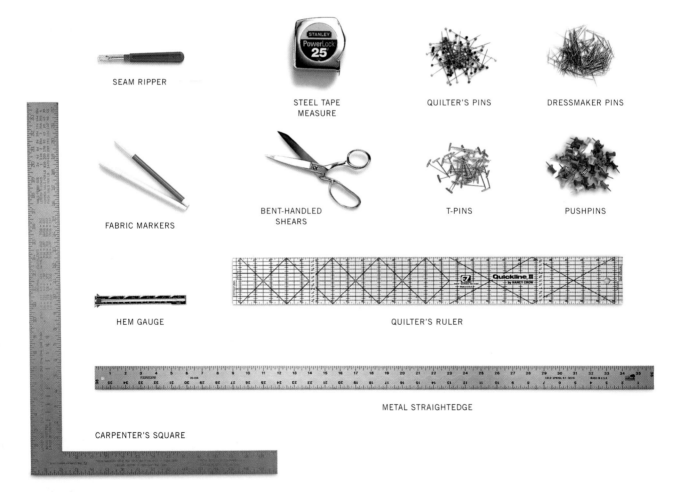

SEAM RIPPER

STEEL TAPE MEASURE

QUILTER'S PINS

DRESSMAKER PINS

FABRIC MARKERS

BENT-HANDLED SHEARS

T-PINS

PUSHPINS

HEM GAUGE

QUILTER'S RULER

METAL STRAIGHTEDGE

CARPENTER'S SQUARE

Sewing window treatments is much easier when you have the right tools and supplies for each step of the way. Essential tools include measuring tools for accuracy, cuttng tools that are sharp and appropriate for the material being cut, a steam iron and ironing accessories, a sewing machine in good working order, and sewing supplies.

square is a lightweight alternative to a carpenter's square.

A metal or wood *straightedge* is useful for marking and extending cutting lines. Available in a variety of sizes, a clear *quilter's grid ruler* at least 18 inches long and 3 inches wide is especially helpful in marking hems.

Handy for measuring and marking fabric, a *cardboard cutting board* or a gridded cutting mat can also be used as a guide when pleating swags.

To mark cutting lines, hems, and pleats, you'll need a *fabric marker*. Your choices are many, from traditional chalk to pens and pencils. Choose a chalk marker that makes a fine, consistent line and does not have to be sharpened. Experiment on your fabric before choosing a marking pen. Some leave permanent marks.

A *hem gauge* is a 6-inch ruler with an adjustable slide that aids in measuring seam allowances and lower and side hems.

CUTTING TOOLS

Easier on the hands than regular scissors, *bent-handled shears* allow the fabric to lie flat while you cut. Choose a lightweight 8- or 9-inch-long pair for quick cutting. To make long, even cuts, you can choose longer *dressmaking shears*.

IRONING TOOLS

A *steam iron* is the most versatile ironing tool because it adjusts conveniently to a wide variety of fabrics. To steam out wrinkles and freshen up window coverings after they're hung, try a *hand steamer*.

Since you'll need a larger surface than most ironing boards offer, consider padding a *large table* or piece of plywood instead (cover the surface as described above).

Keep a *plastic spray bottle* handy near the ironing surface for extra

---

PADDING A WORK SURFACE

Covering your work surface with padding prevents your fabric from slipping and sliding and allows you to anchor the fabric as you're working.

COVERING A TABLE. *Drape enough cotton (not polyester) batting on the table so you have at least a ½-inch thickness. Starting at one end, pull the corners tightly and fasten them underneath with safety pins. Repeat at the other end. Tape any dangling edges.*

Cover the padding with an unpatterned cotton sheet, muslin or canvas. Smooth and fasten as you did the batting. Spray the surface with water; as the fabric dries, it will shrink over the padding.

PADDING A PLYWOOD SHEET OR A DOOR. *Begin by laying a cotton sheet, muslin or canvas on the floor and layering cotton batting on the fabric to a thickness of ½ inch. Center the plywood or door on top. Starting at the middle of one long side, fold the batting and fabric over the edge and secure every 2 inches using a staple gun. Repeat to staple the opposite side, pulling tautly. Do the same on the remaining sides.*

Return to the starting point and continue pulling and stapling the batting and fabric in 12-inch segments on both sides of the center until you've worked to the corners. Miter the corners and staple. Dampen as described above.

---

moisture. Always test a sample of your fabric first to avoid water spotting.

SEWING TOOLS

Your *sewing machine* needs to be in good working order. Clean and oil it before every project. Have it serviced professionally once a year. A serger or overlock machine is not essential, but it certainly saves time in finishing edges and makes your work look more professional.

A strip of *masking tape* laid down on the throat plate of your sewing machine serves as a handy guide for keeping seams and hems straight. For hints on using tape, see page 25.

Always use *sewing machine needles* that are compatible with the weight of your fabric. The heavier the fabric and number of layers of fabric, the higher the number on the needle. Use an 80/12 for medium-weight fabrics, a 70/10 for sheer fabrics, and

a 90/14 or above for heavy fabrics and for tacking pleats. Change to a new needle at the start of every project.

A packet of *hand-sewing needles* in assorted sizes should take care of most hand-sewing jobs. But tacking pleats by hand will require an especially heavy-duty needle.

Fine, sharp *dressmaker pins* number 20, 1¼ inches long, are best to use. Glass heads on the pins prevent melting when near an iron. And remember to always remove pins before sewing over them.

Stronger than dressmaker pins are *T-pins,* useful for holding plush or open-weave fabrics. T-pins come in size 20 and size 24 (large). *Pushpins* are useful for holding pleats on swags and temporarily securing shades, valances, swags, and cascades to mounting boards.

A fine, sharp *seam ripper* speeds the task of taking out any imperfect rows of stitching.

window math

The key to making treatments that fit your windows perfectly is careful measuring and calculating. It's a challenging but critical job—a miscalculation of even an inch or two could leave you short yards of fabric. The instructions in this section will guide you.

Read the following sequence to get a feel for the entire process involved in making window treatments. Then you will be ready to measure your window and determine the yardage needed for your project.

Choose your window treatment project and the type of fabric from which you'll make it (see the next chapter for projects and pages 21–23 for fabric guidelines).

Decide on the type of hardware you'll use (for hardware information on your particular treatment, look at the project chapter starting on page 29). Purchase the hardware after you've measured your windows, but don't install it until after your project is completed.

Measure your windows according to the instructions that follow, and record the measurements in the spaces provided in the window diagram (right). Guidelines are included to help you determine how much coverage you need above, below, and on the sides of the window.

Fill in the window treatment work sheet on page 18 to determine the yardage required. (The work sheet applies to all treatments except swags and cornices; you'll find measuring and calculating instructions for those treatments in the project section.) Fill in every box that applies; put a slash through those that don't.

Purchase the fabric and any trimmings and notions.

Make the window treatment, determine where on the window it goes, and install the hardware and treatment.

the professional approach to measuring

This approach, used by professionals, works directly from the window measurements rather than from the hardware.

TAKING WINDOW MEASUREMENTS

Measuring a window opening is straight-forward (see drawing below). Be sure to use a steel tape when measuring and write in the spaces provided.

If your treatment will be mounted inside the window, you need measure only the width of the opening (A) and the length (B). But if your treatment will hang outside the opening, as most do, you'll have to determine not only the width and length of the opening but also the area to be covered to the left (C) and right (D) of the opening and from the top (E) and bottom (F).

Extensions depend on how much light control and privacy you want (see page 9). For treatments that, when opened, don't clear the window completely, extensions can range from 2 to 10 inches. For draperies that traverse to open completely, see the information on stackback on the facing page.

Shades usually extend ½ inch beyond the trim board on each side or 2 inches beyond the window opening if there's no trim. If treatments are being teamed, the extensions must be sufficient to allow the top treatment hardware to clear the undertreatment at the top and sides.

The top of window treatments is usually even with the top of the trim board. You may also begin a treatment just below the ceiling, at the bottom of crown molding, or halfway between the ceiling and window opening. Valances typically begin 8 inches above the opening.

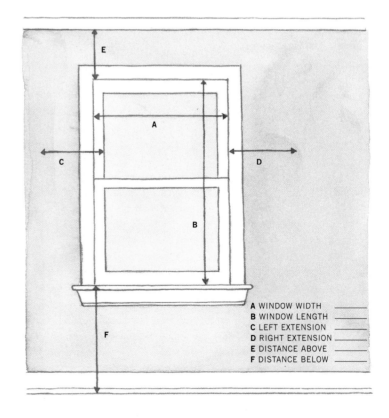

A WINDOW WIDTH _____
B WINDOW LENGTH _____
C LEFT EXTENSION _____
D RIGHT EXTENSION _____
E DISTANCE ABOVE _____
F DISTANCE BELOW _____

Treatments are generally most pleasing when they end in line with either the window or floor. Floor-length treatments should end ½ inch short of the floor. There are two exceptions: If you use an open-weave fabric or live in a particularly humid area, end the treatment 1 inch above the floor. In double treatments, the inner treatment should be ½ inch shorter than the outer one.

USING EXISTING HARDWARE

If the hardware already on your windows is in good condition and meets your needs, you can reuse it. Take the following measurements and use them to fill in the window treatment work sheet on page 18.

1 Measure rod or pole from end to end for rod or pole size.

2 Measure from front of hardware to wall for return. For draperies, measure the center overlap when the treatment is closed.

3 *For rod-pocket curtains* or *valances,* measure from top of rod or pole to where treatment will end; add desired depth of heading, if used. Add take-up allowance (see page 19, step 7). To ensure correct length, pin or baste hem. Then stitch final hem.
For tab curtains, measurements will depend on length of tab.
For draperies on a standard traverse rod, measure from top of rod to floor; subtract ½ inch. *For draperies on a decorative rod,* measure from bottom of rod or rings to where treatment will end. *For curtains on rings,* measure from bottom of rings to where treatment will end.

PUDDLING

A designer detail called puddling is a dramatic way to end draperies and curtains at the floor. Add from 10 to 12 inches to the finished floor length. Use crisp fabrics such as silk douppioni or linen for the right look.

ALLOWING FOR STACKBACK

Curtains or draperies that open to expose the entire glass area—or most of it—need room to stack beyond the glass. This area is called the stackback.

For most fabrics you'll need to allow one-third the width of the glass area (or the area you wish to expose) for the stackback. For a two-way draw treatment, place half the stackback on each side of the glass. For a one-way draw, the entire stackback goes on one side.

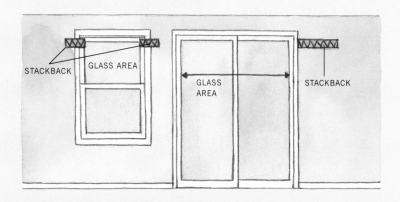

WINDOW TREATMENT WORK SHEET

NUMBER OF WIDTHS

Left Extension	Window Width	Right Extension	Rod, Pole, or Board Size	Return + Overlap* + Return	Finished Width	Fullness	Side Hems	Total Width Required	Usable Fabric Width	Number of Widths
+	+	=	+	=	x	+	=	÷	=	

*FOR DRAPERIES ONLY

TOTAL YARDS

Distance Above	Window Length	Distance Below	Finished Length	Top Allowance	Hem	1" Ravel Allowance	Cut Length or Repeat Cut Length	Number of Widths	Required Fabric in Inches	Inches Converted to Yards	Yards Needed
+	+	=	+	+	+	=	x	=	÷ 36	=	

LINING

Finished Length* + 5"*	Number of Widths	Inches Converted to Yards	Yards Needed
x	÷ 36	=	

*FOR CURTAINS AND DRAPERIES ONLY; FOR OTHER TREATMENTS, SEE INDIVIDUAL PROJECTS.

RETURN SIZE CHART

Treatments on Window	Return Size*
1 Treatment	3$^1/_2$"
2 Treatments	5$^1/_2$"
3 Treatments	7$^1/_2$"

*MAY VARY; CHECK MANUFACTURER'S INSTRUCTIONS.

yardage calculations

Though the process may seem laborious, only careful calculating will ensure that you'll have sufficient fabric to complete your project. Using the window measurements you just made, follow the steps below, filling in the window treatment sheet as you go.

To determine allowances for fullness, hems, headings, and pockets, turn to the project you're making (see the next chapter) and look under "Calculating Yardage."

DETERMINING NUMBER OF WIDTHS

Number of widths is determined by adding amounts needed for side hems and fullness to the finished width of the treatment as it will hang, closed, at the window.

1 Add left extension, width of window opening, and right extension to get rod, pole, or board size.

2 To that figure, add returns—distance from front of hardware to wall—and overlap.

For return size for one or more treatments on a single window, see the chart above. For traversing draperies only, add 1$^1/_2$ inches to each panel for the overlap.

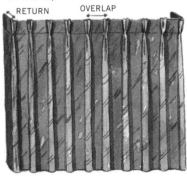

RETURN   OVERLAP

3 Multiply finished width by desired fullness, usually 2½ times for medium-weight fabrics and 3 times for sheers.

4 Add side hem allowances for total width required.

5 Divide total width by fabric width to arrive at number of widths needed. Most fabrics and linings are 48 to 54 inches wide. If lining is different than fabric, calculate number of lining widths separately.

Sheers, often 118 inches wide, are meant to be fabricated without seams, with selvages running parallel to floor. This is called "railroading." In this case, divide total width by 36 inches for yardage.

6 If number of widths determined in step 5 isn't a whole number, round it off. For any treatment with horizontal fullness, round off to next whole number if fractional part is ½ or greater (for example, 3.7 widths rounds off to 4); round off to smaller whole number if fractional part is less than ½. If your number is 1 plus any fraction, round up to 2; otherwise, you would split one width.

Most curtains and draperies open at center; each half of the treatment is called a panel. When you have two panels, divide total number of fabric widths in half to determine how many widths will make up each panel. For example, a pair of draperies that requires 5 widths of fabric will have 2½ widths in each panel. With draperies, never use less than half a width (anything narrower is difficult to pleat).

For Roman or roller shades, always round up to the next full width.

DETERMINING TOTAL YARDAGE FOR UNPATTERNED FABRIC

Total yardage is based on cut length (the finished length plus headings, hems, and a ravel allowance) multiplied by the number of widths. For information on calculating cut length and total yardage for patterned fabric, see below.

Continue on the second line of the work sheet.

7 Add length of window opening to distance above and below opening to arrive at finished length.

For curtains on flat rods, add ½ inch to finished length to allow for take-up (1 inch total on a sash curtain); *for wide, flat rods*, add 1 inch; *for round rods*, add rod diameter.

8 To finished length, add top allowance and lower hem allowance (see individual project for specific figures) plus a 1-inch ravel allowance to get cut length.

9 Multiply cut length by number of widths to get total length in inches. Divide result by 36 to arrive at number of yards to buy. Add about 5 percent more (a minimum of 1 yard) for flaws.

DETERMINING TOTAL YARDAGE FOR PATTERNED FABRIC

If you plan to use a fabric with a printed or woven design, you'll probably have to buy extra yardage since, with few exceptions, the repeats in the pattern must be matched when you make your window treatment.

The calculations are the same as those for unpatterned fabric up to the cut length figure. It's this measurement that needs to be adjusted to account for the pattern repeat on your fabric.

MUST PATTERNS MATCH? A tiny pattern repeat—a dot or small floral pattern, for example—may not need to be matched for gathered styles, such as rod-pocket curtains. But don't let the size of the repeat fool you. Even the smallest patterns can look mismatched after the fabric has been seamed.

To see if small repeats will need matching, unroll enough yardage while you're in the store so you can lay two sections of the fabric side by side, selvages aligned. Matching motifs in the pattern, arrange the fabric sections to make the pattern continue across the two widths. Now shift one of the sections slightly.

If you can't see any difference in the pattern, you can calculate total yardage according to the directions for unpatterned fabrics. But if the pattern fluctuates jarringly, base your calculations on the size of the pattern repeat (see below).

MEASURING THE REPEAT. To calculate the extra yardage for matching patterns, you must measure and record the height of the pattern repeat, called the vertical repeat.

Vertical repeat. Measure lengthwise from the same spot on one motif within the repeat to the same spot in the next identical motif. That distance is the vertical repeat.

VERTICAL REPEAT

Matching widths. Most patterned fabric is designed so that horizontal repeats match at the selvages or just inside them.

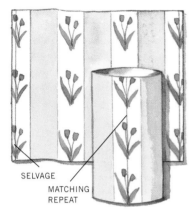

SELVAGE
MATCHING REPEAT

If the pattern matches farther into the width, you'll lose fabric when you stitch widths together. Check to see where patterned fabric matches before you buy it. If the distance from the inner edge of the selvage to the point where you'll stitch is more than an inch, don't buy the fabric.

Pattern placement. To make seams inconspicuous, repeats on each fabric width should match those on adjoining widths, repeats on each panel should match, and the pattern on all the windows in the room should also match.

You have some flexibility in where the pattern repeats fall on the finished treatment. The usual approach is to place full repeats at the lower hem and allow the top of the treatment to end anywhere on the repeat. If you place the top of a full repeat at the top of the treatment, the pattern will be lost in the pleats or gathers.

When treatments are different at the top or bottom, place a full repeat at the bottom of the longest treatment. On the shorter treatment, place the pattern so the eye reads the repeats at the same level in all treatments.

REPEAT CUT LENGTH AND YARDAGE CALCULATIONS. To adjust the cut length for your pattern repeat and determine total yardage, follow the steps below.

1 Follow directions for steps 1–8 on pages 18–19.

2 Divide cut-length measurement by vertical repeat size. Round up to next whole number if result contains a fraction to arrive at number of pattern repeats needed for each cut length.

3 Multiply that number by vertical repeat to determine, in inches, repeat cut length.

4 Multiply repeat cut length by number of fabric widths to get total length in inches. Divide by 36 to convert to yards.

Those few crucial inches. To make sure that pattern repeats will fall in the right place when your window treatment is made up, it's crucial to start measuring total yardage at the correct point in the pattern, rather than at the cut end of the yardage on the bolt. Usually, the cut end coming off the bolt is the bottom of the pattern, that is, the motifs run toward the center of the bolt. Study the pattern and look for arrows on the selvage to determine which way is up.

To have full repeats fall at the bottom of the treatment, unroll enough yardage to find the full repeat that would end at the lower fold. Measure below that for the hem allowance; begin to measure total yardage there.

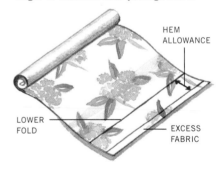

HEM ALLOWANCE
LOWER FOLD
EXCESS FABRIC

ADDING LININGS AND INTERLININGS

The benefits of lining window treatments far outweigh the added cost and time. A lining increases insulation, provides a greater degree of privacy, and extends the life of the window treatment by protecting the face fabric. It also improves the appearance of window treatments both on the inside and outside of your home.

Most lining fabrics are made of cotton, cotton/polyester, or polyester/rayon blends. Sateen, a type of strong, tightly woven fabric, comes in white and a range of off-whites. For a uniform appearance from the outside, use the same color lining for all window treatments.

For energy efficiency and light control, you can use insulating (also called thermal) and blackout linings, which are lining fabrics that have been laminated with vinyl or layered with foam acrylic.

Cotton flannel is often used to interline a window treatment, adding body and insulating qualities as well as blocking noise and light. An interlining fabric is cut to the same size as the face fabric and basted together with it around all the edges before the window treatment construction begins. The face fabric and interlining are then used as one fabric.

selecting and preparing fabric

Crucial to the success of a window treatment is the fabric from which it's made. But selecting a suitable fabric from the dizzying array available in fabric stores and sample books can be tiring and frustrating. That's why it's important to know what to look for in a fabric and how to prepare it so it will hang evenly and drape smoothly.

shopping tips

You'll find the best fabric selection, as well as the most knowledgeable salespeople, in stores that specialize in fabrics for home decorating. Other good sources include full-service fabric stores, which often have home decorating fabric sections, and interior decorators and designers, who have access to fabrics from many sources.

LOOKING AT FABRIC

Choosing fabric involves more than simply picking a color or pattern that you like. Here are some guidelines.

APPEARANCE. Undoubtedly, your first consideration as you browse among the bolts of fabric will be appearance. When you shop, take along paint chips and fabric swatches to compare colors, textures, and patterns with those of your walls and furnishings.

Because background color and lighting can alter a fabric's appearance, try to take an entire bolt of fabric home with you for a day or two. Or buy a yard of fabric and hang it at the window you're planning to cover. Check for ease of sewing, and whether it wrinkles easily or shows water spots.

When you are in the store, unroll several yards and gather one end in your hand. Does it drape well? Does it have the necessary weight for the treatment you're considering? Does the design or texture hold its own, without getting lost in the folds?

Stand back several feet so you can see how the fabric looks from a distance.

GRAIN. To drape properly, fabric must have as straight a grain as possible, that is, its crosswise threads should run perpendicular to its lengthwise threads.

The selvage is parallel to the lengthwise grain. You will need to establish the crosswise grain. This can be accomplished by clipping into the selvage and tearing the fabric from selvage to selvage. If the fabric does not tear easily, then clip the fabric past the selvage and draw out a thread as far as possible until it breaks. Cut along the space that is created. Draw out another strand of thread and continue cutting.

Be very careful when selecting a patterned fabric. The less expensive the fabric, the more likely that the print will be slightly off-grain, veering at an angle from the crosswise threads. Usually, the misalignment isn't severe enough to be noticeable. But if you're not sure about the pattern, take a closer look.

To check patterned fabric, fold the fabric back a few inches, wrong side in, aligning the selvages. If the print runs evenly along the fold, it's fairly well aligned with the fabric grain. But if it wanders across the fold, the print is badly off-grain. Because it's virtually impossible to straighten the grain, don't buy any fabric on which the pattern is off by more than ½ inch in each width.

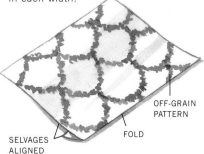

SELVAGES ALIGNED

OFF-GRAIN PATTERN

FOLD

FINISHES. Finishes added to fabrics prevent wrinkles and mildew and discourage insects. The most appreciated finishes, however, are those that repel stains and soil. Silicone finishes seal fibers, allowing you to wipe away water-based stains. Fluorochemical finishes repel both water and oil-based stains and last through several dry cleanings. Note that some finishes make the fabric more difficult to sew.

BUYING AND PREPARING FABRIC

Once you've selected your fabric, buy all you need at one time (plus an extra ½ yard for sample pressing and stitching). If possible, buy all the fabric from one bolt. If the amount of fabric left on a bolt is too little for your project, special-order a full bolt.

CHECKING DYE LOTS. Most fabrics are marked with a dye lot number on the store tag. If you're using fabric from two different dye lots, hold the fabrics together and examine them in different light; look for any perceptible differences in the colors. If you can't see any, you're probably safe.

But to ensure the best results, don't mix fabric from different bolts at the same window. For example, if you have three windows, buy enough from one bolt to make treatments for two of them; then, from another bolt, buy all of the fabric for the third window. To do this, you'll need to think in terms of cut lengths instead of total yardage when the fabric is being measured. Mark the pieces so you won't mix them up while you're sewing.

INSPECTING FABRIC FOR FLAWS. If you're buying fabric off a bolt, hold it up to the light and inspect it for small holes or inconsistencies in the weave. Sometimes, flaws are marked along the selvage with tape or pins.

Ask to have extra fabric to allow for the flaws or choose not to purchase the fabric. Always buy 5 percent more fabric (a minimum of 1 yard) to account for any flaws.

PRESHRINKING AND CLEANING YOUR FABRIC.

It is generally not a good idea to preshrink home decorating fabric. Preshrinking can wash away the fabric's protective finish and cause it to lose its fresh, crisp appearance.

As a rule, it's a good idea to dry-clean treatments made from home decorating fabrics. Unlined curtains are about the only treatment that may be successfully laundered.

CHOOSING THREAD

All-purpose 100 percent cotton thread works well for all fabrics and blends. Polyester thread is sometimes used for synthetic fabrics, but it stretches slightly when sewn and has a tendency to pucker.

When matching thread to fabric, choose thread that's a slightly darker shade than the fabric. For prints, match the thread to the background or the most predominant color. Use the same thread color for serging and finishing edges.

how to cut lengths

To cut your fabric into the lengths required for your project, you'll need the cut length or repeat cut length measurement from your window treatment work sheet (see page 18); a large, flat work surface; a carpenter's square or a matte board; a straightedge; and chalk or a fabric marker. Use one of the following methods, depending on whether your fabric is unpatterned or patterned.

UNPATTERNED FABRIC

For fabric with no discernible pattern, you'll need to square off one cut end of the yardage; then you can begin cutting lengths.

SQUARING OFF THE FABRIC. To begin, lay the fabric, right side up, on a flat surface.

A good way to create a cutting guide is to pull a crosswise thread, if possible. Cut into the fabric beyond the selvage near one cut end. Pick up one thread and pull it across the width. If the thread breaks, cut farther into the fabric next to the thread and pick it up again.

If you couldn't pull a thread, align the short blade of the square along one selvage of the fabric, close to one cut end, at the point where you'll be able to mark a line across the full width of the fabric. Using the other blade of the square as a straightedge, draw a line perpendicular to the selvage.

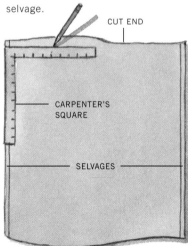

CUT END

CARPENTER'S SQUARE

SELVAGES

Remove the square and use a straightedge to extend the line 12 inches at a time to the opposite selvage. With the square, check that the line meets the opposite selvage at a perfect right angle. Cut along the line.

CUTTING LENGTHS. Measure down each selvage a distance equal to the cut length; clip selvages at this point. Using a straightedge, draw a line across the fabric between the clips. With a carpenter's square, check each corner for squareness.

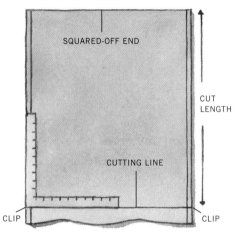

SQUARED-OFF END

CUT LENGTH

CUTTING LINE

CLIP

CLIP

Cut along the line; this is the first squared-off length.

Continue to measure, mark, and cut until all lengths are cut. To avoid sewing one width to another upside down, make a small notch in the selvage at the lower right corner of each length.

PATTERNED FABRIC

Many prints and some woven pattern repeats run slightly off-grain. When you cut print fabric for window treatments, follow the lines of the pattern rather than the grain of the fabric.

Once all the widths have been seamed, you can then square off the bottom edge.

SQUARING OFF FIRST END. On a flat surface, lay out several yards of fabric, wrong side up. At the cut end, bring the selvages together in the center, forming a tube. Look to see where the motifs—a flower, a leaf, a geometric shape—match.

Mark the matching points on each selvage where you started measuring total yardage when you bought the fabric. Unfold the fabric, turn it right side up, and, using a straightedge, connect the marks to make your cutting line. Cut along this line.

CUTTING LENGTHS. To cut the first length, follow the instructions for unpatterned fabric (see page 22), substituting your repeat cut-length figure for the cut length.

To cut additional lengths, tape the uncut fabric down, right side up. Lay the first cut length, right side up, on top, carefully positioning it so the motifs in the pattern repeats match perfectly.

Mark the cutting point on each selvage; remove the top piece and use a straightedge to mark the cutting line. Then cut along the marked line. Repeat for each successive length.

To avoid confusion when you sew widths together, mark pieces by making a small notch in the selvage at the lower right corner of each length.

SQUARING OFF JOINED WIDTHS. If, after joining widths, the top and bottom edges aren't square, you'll need to square and trim the bottom. The top edge will be squared when you measure and mark the hem, the finished length, and the top allowance.

With the panel right side up, lay a carpenter's square along the selvage on the short edge. Mark a line perpendicular to the selvage; extend the line 12 inches at a time to keep it straight. You'll have a triangular segment left at the bottom.

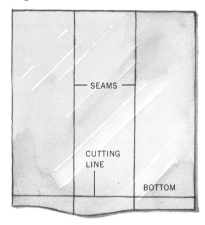

Before you cut on the marked line, be sure you will have enough fabric at the top. With some patterned fabrics, the repeat cut length will provide the extra fabric you'll need to square the bottom and still give you the required inches at the top.

Measure the hem allowance plus the finished length from the marked line. From this point, measure the top allowance and check to be sure that it doesn't go beyond the shorter edge. If it does extend beyond, you'll need to decrease slightly the depth of your hem and/or heading.

TRIMMING SELVAGES. Some selvages are woven tighter than the fabric and tend to draw up. If your fabric is unpatterned, trim the selvages before joining widths. With some patterned fabrics, the pattern matches so close to the selvages that seam allowances will be reduced if you trim the selvages first. If the selvages and fabric lie flat, you do not need to trim the selvages.

JOINING AND TRIMMING FABRIC WIDTHS. For a neat appearance, full widths of fabric should hang at the leading edge of a treatment. Place partial widths on the sides. For draperies, a partial width must be at least half a width. On a single panel treatment, center a full width.

For an unpatterned fabric, join widths with $1/2$-inch seams. For a perfect match on patterned fabric, lay widths right sides together with selvages aligned. Fold back the selvage edges until the pattern matches exactly. Press the fold lightly.

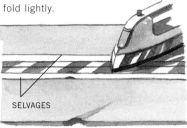

Unfold the selvage edges, pin the layers, and stitch on the fold.

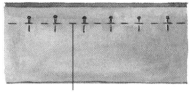

STITCH ALONG FOLD

After seaming widths, trim the panel to the total width required.

Sewing window treatments is about as simple as sewing can be. Here are a few basic techniques that will help speed the work.

hand-sewing techniques

Hand sewing is used for temporary stitching or for finishing. Use a single, rather than double, strand of thread and wax it for better control. For temporary stitching, do not knot the thread; secure it with a couple of small stitches instead.

If you are left-handed, reverse the terms *right* and *left* in the following directions.

SLIPSTITCH. The slipstitch provides an almost invisible finish for hems, linings, and trims. Working from right to left, insert the needle into the folded edge of the upper layer, slide it inside the fold, bring it out 1/8 to 1/4 inch from the insertion point, and then slide the needle under a single thread of the lower layer. Repeat. When slipstitching braids or other trims, slide the needle through and along the woven or twisted edge, concealing the thread.

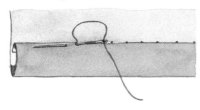

BLINDSTITCH. The blindstitch is used for hemming and holding facings in place, and is inconspicuous on both sides. First, finish the cut edge of the hem or facing. Roll this edge back about 1/4 inch. Working from right to left, make a small horizontal stitch under one thread of the fabric, then under a thread of the hem or facing diagonally opposite the first stitch.

CATCHSTITCH. The catchstitch holds two overlapping layers of fabric in place while allowing some flexibility in their alignment. Use it to attach raw or finished edges of hems and facings to the wrong side of fabrics. Work from left to right, but insert the needle from right to left. Make a small horizontal stitch in one layer, then make a second stitch diagonally opposite the first in the other layer. Repeat, alternating stitches along the edge in a zigzag fashion and keeping the threads loose.

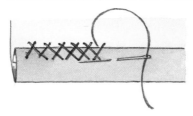

machine-sewing techniques

The directions in this book call for a variety of machine stitches including finishing edges and seams, hems, and topstitching. All are explained below.

SERGED EDGE OR SEAM. A serger produces an overlocking stitch to prevent raveling and, at the same time, trims excess fabric from the seam allowance. A three-thread stitch formation is commonly used as an edge finish. A four-thread stitch formation can seam and finish in one pass.

ZIGZAG EDGE AND SEAM. A zigzag stitch sewn along the raw edge of a fabric allows it to lie flat and prevents raveling. Center presser foot over raw edge of your fabric and zigzag-stitch, allowing needle to stitch both on and off fabric an even distance.

A zigzag seam is a sturdy, ravel-proof seam. Place the fabric right sides together. Stitch on the seamline, using a narrow, short zigzag, 1mm wide and 1mm long. In the seam allowance, stitch another zigzag, 2mm wide and 2mm long. Trim the excess seam allowance. This seam is especially useful on loosely woven and stretchy fabrics.

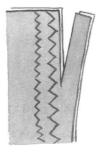

DOUBLE HEM. Both side and lower hems are doubled to make the treatment hang better. For most projects, the lower hem goes in before the side hems.

To make a double hem, turn up the lower edge of the hem allowance, wrong sides together, and press. Turn the raw edge in to meet the pressed fold and press again. Hem by hand or machine close to the second fold.

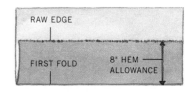

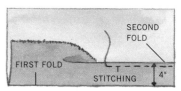

Repeat for the lining, adjusting the first fold to the total hem allowance.

Make a double side hem in the same way, using the total side hem allowances as the guide for the first fold. Hand-stitch the opening closed at the lower edge.

If a fabric has a loose weave or is particularly heavy, it may stretch after hanging. Instead of stitching the hem, baste it and hang the treatment for a week or so. Then adjust the hem and stitch.

MITER ADJOINING HEMS. With this method, you can miter adjoining hems whether symmetrical or asymmetrical.

Mark and press adjacent hems in place. Mark intersection where hem edges meet, placing a pin in the fold of each hem. Mark lower corner with pin.

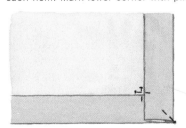

Open out the folds, keeping the pins in place. Turn hem, right sides together, keeping the first fold turned under and matching the pins. Mark a diagonal line from the pins on folded edges to the corner pin. (Fabric edges will line up for a symmetrical miter but not for an asymmetrical miter.) Stitch along marked line.

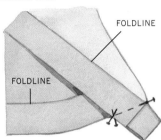

Before trimming the seam, turn the corner right side out to be sure it's correct. Then turn back and trim seam allowance to $\frac{1}{4}$ inch. Finger-press seam allowance open, turn right side out, and press again. Topstitch hems in place.

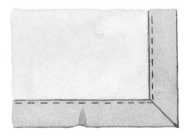

WEIGHTS. Weights sewn into the lower corners of each panel and at each seam make full-length panels hang straighter. Either purchase covered weights or enclose weights in small pockets of fabric.

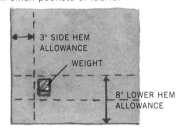

3" SIDE HEM ALLOWANCE

WEIGHT

8" LOWER HEM ALLOWANCE

BLINDHEM. Most sewing machines come with a blindhem presser foot that makes a perfect hidden stitch. After pressing the hem to the wrong side, fold the project away from the hem, exposing about $\frac{1}{4}$ inch of the wrong side of the hem edge. Align the presser foot guide blade along the fold of the project and set the machine to a blindhem stitch. The needle will sew about five stitches on the hem only and then cross over with a zigzag stitch to catch the project. Check your sewing machine guide book for exact settings.

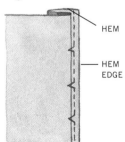

HEM

HEM EDGE

TOPSTITCH. Topstitching can be decorative, functional, or both. Using a regular stitch length, stitch through one or more layers of fabric with the face fabric right side up in the machine. To ensure accuracy, baste from the wrong side first and topstitch on the right side using the basting as a guide.

Marking the line with chalk on the right side also helps in stitching a straight line.

A TAPE TRICK

Masking tape can help keep seams and hems straight and parallel.

For a seam guide, measure to the right of the needle a distance equal to the seam allowance. On the machine, place a strip of tape with the left edge at this point, parallel to the stitching line. As you sew, keep the seam allowance aligned with the tape's edge.

For a hem guide, measure $\frac{1}{8}$ inch less than hem width; tape. This way, the stitches will run just inside the inner fold of the hem.

a fabric collection

Fabric, whether made from a natural fiber or a synthetic, is the key to a beautiful window covering. Good fabric drapes well, pleats crisply, and has more body—all characteristics of a professional-looking window treatment.

SHEER

Sheer fabrics, with their open weaves and delicate yarns, filter light and offer privacy. Cotton, linen, and polyester are fibers commonly used in sheer fabrics.

MEDIUM-WEIGHT

Medium-weight fabrics are favorites with home sewers because they are easy to handle. From plain linen weaves to bold chintzes, from striped sheeting to convenient blends, medium-weight fabrics are the most versatile choice for many styles.

HEAVYWEIGHT

Sumptuous satins and silks and full-bodied cottons and rayon velvets make elegant drapery panels that can be used in a variety of rooms from casual to formal.

MIXING AND MATCHING

The best-dressed windows often feature fabrics that combine patterns and textures. You can use plaids and stripes, florals and checks, in coordinating or contrasting colors to create interest and enhance a room. The coordinating fabric lines offered by today's manufacturers make it easier than ever to mix and match fabrics. Bows, tassels, fringe, and matching fabric rosettes are the jewelry that accessorizes the final look.

window treatment projects

With the availability of beautiful fabrics and a variety of hardware styles, it's now not only practical to sew your own window treatments, it's fun, too. And even more important, creating the right window treatment will enhance a room as well as reflect your personal taste.

Look through the window treatment projects on the following pages and you'll find instructions for a variety of coverings from easy-to-make rod-pocket curtains to formal layers of swags and cascades. To make them, all you need is a sewing machine, some good tools, and a desire to create a unique window covering.

ABOVE: White gauze tab curtains loosely mounted on wrought iron rods soften these living room windows without hindering the view. The leaf finials add a dramatic touch.

RIGHT: A tab-topped gingham curtain hung from knobs becomes a stationary window treatment. A roller shade provides light control so the curtain can be permanently tied back for effect. The tieback is made of the same decorative cord as the tabs.

The alternating colors used in these knotted tab curtains add a fashion flair to a light and bright "outdoor" room. Using the same color tabs on all the panels provides an unexpected touch.

curtains

ABOVE: Sheer curtains banded and tabbed in a contrasting transparent fabric float in the breeze, while the added length allows the panels to puddle gracefully on the floor. A matching wrapped swag adds a touch of formality to the treatment.

RIGHT: A simple rod-pocket curtain in a light and airy sheer completes this traditional country bathroom. The use of a narrow rod pocket allows the fabric to take center stage.

LEFT: Sheer rod-pocket panels hung on a retro-style, gold-leaf wood rod with bold finials complement the bright, contemporary furnishings in this comfortable corner reading nook.

BELOW: Sash curtains take on a new look when used in elegant Palladian-style windows. The translucent white fabric affords some privacy while allowing the architectural punch of the windows its full power.

OPPOSITE: Casually dressed and puddled on the floor, these flat panels constructed in a burn-out, tone-on-tone sheer fabric are clipped to metal rings on a funky rod. The spiral finials repeat the circles in the fabric pattern.

LEFT: Country casual print curtains in this breakfast room are sewn to oversized bright red wood rings that contrast with the large white wood rod mounted at the ceiling.

BELOW: Tailored and precise, these heavy cotton-and-rayon curtain panels are attached to a decorative metal rod with large eyelets inserted at regular intervals into the heading.

how to make curtains

Today's curtains offer a myriad of style possibilities, from elegant full-length panels softly swagged and tied to simple sash or tailored tab curtains. The projects offered here reflect the diversity of curtain styles and looks. Best of all, you'll discover that curtains are easy—and fun—to make.

a look at hardware

Your curtain hardware needs to complement the fabric you're planning to use, as well as the style of the curtains and rooms where they'll hang. Look for hardware in discount and department stores, home improvement centers, and large fabric stores that specialize in home decorating fabrics. Most curtain hardware from these sources is manufactured by just two or three companies. For something more unusual, shop through mail-order sources, consult an interior decorator, or look for shops specializing in decorative hardware.

For examples of curtain hardware, see below right and facing page.

RODS AND POLES

Most rods are adjustable; most wood poles are not. Generally, both rods and poles rest in brackets attached to the wall or window frame.

Rounded *café rods*, available in a range of sizes, styles, and finishes, are designated for café or full-length curtains that are gathered on the rod or hung on rings.

Flat curtain rods, either single or double, hold lightweight rod-pocket curtains or valances that are either gathered on the rod or hung on oval rings or hooks. If you're using a sheer fabric for rod-pocket curtains, look for clear rods that won't show through the fabric. Flexible clear rods are used for sunburst curtains.

For corner or bay windows, choose adjustable hinged flat or decorative rods, also called swing rods or portiere rods.

Wide flat rods, available in 2$\frac{1}{2}$- and 4$\frac{1}{2}$-inch widths, require an extra-wide rod pocket, adding visual depth and interest to traditional curtain styles.

Sash rods attach with shallow brackets to the top and bottom of the window frame. Flat or round sash rods are commonly used on French doors and casement windows to hold sash or hourglass curtains.

Oval or round *tension rods* have a spring-tension mechanism to hold the plastic- or rubber-tipped rod within the window frame. Often, they're the only practical choice for recessed windows. Support a width greater than 36 inches with cup hooks.

Wood poles, used with decorative brackets and finials, lend distinction to rod-pocket or tab curtains. With the addition of matching wood rings, poles are also suitable for flat curtain panels.

Sleek, contemporary *cable rods* consist of a twisted wire cable that is cut to measure, streamlined rings, and end support brackets. This system's minimalist look works well in contemporary applications.

ACCESSORIES

Many of the following accessories can be found where curtain hardware is sold or in the notions section of stores that carry home decorating fabrics.

Finials are decorative end pieces that attach to the ends of poles that aren't mitered or finished with elbows.

Small and unobtrusive *wood sockets* hold wood poles in inside-mounted installations. The sockets are screwed into the window frame.

To increase the length of the rod return, attach *extension plates* to ordinary brackets.

Rings for curtains have small eyelets or clips on the bottom. They can be sewn or clipped to the top edge of a curtain, but you'll have to remove them before dry-cleaning the treatment. If the eyelets are large enough, you can use them in combination with 1-inch drapery hooks; pin the hooks to the back of the curtain heading and slip through the eyelets.

Valance hooks, designed for stationary treatments, fit over rods.

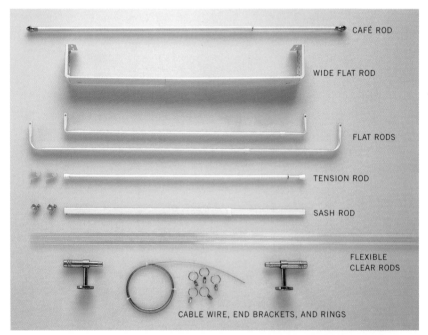

CAFÉ ROD

WIDE FLAT ROD

FLAT RODS

TENSION ROD

SASH ROD

FLEXIBLE CLEAR RODS

CABLE WIRE, END BRACKETS, AND RINGS

These curtain rods hold sheer and lightweight treatments. The cable rod system can support a light- to medium-weight curtain but is limited in the length it can span.

Jumbo grommets or eyelets provide an opening through which a rod is inserted. With this system of attachment, rod pockets or rings are not required.

hardware installation

Mount your hardware only *after* you've completed your project. Follow the manufacturer's instructions for the best results.

Where you'll install the hardware depends on the coverage you planned for when you calculated your yardage. Referring to your window treatment work sheet (see page 18), find the side extensions you allowed and mark those points at the window opening.

If your curtain has no heading, the top of the rod goes at the distance above the window opening noted on your work sheet. For a curtain with a heading, subtract the heading size from the distance the treatment extends above the opening. For example, if you planned to cover 5 inches above the window opening and your heading measures 2 inches, the top of the rod goes 3 inches above the opening.

To determine where to position the brackets, place the rod in a bracket and measure the distance from the top of the rod to the top screw hole in the bracket; add this distance to the previous figure and mark this point at the top of the window opening.

Install one bracket, attaching the top screw at the point you just marked. Place one end of the rod in the bracket and have a helper hold up the other end in its bracket. Before attaching the second bracket, check the rod with a carpenter's level. When the rod is level, mark the top screw hole for the second bracket and screw it to the wall.

If you're not able to screw into the studs, use expansion bolts, also called molly bolts. Plastic anchors are good for lightweight treatments or when you're installing concealed tieback holders.

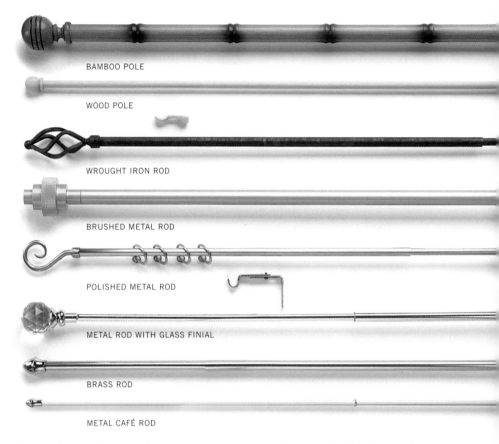

BAMBOO POLE

WOOD POLE

WROUGHT IRON ROD

BRUSHED METAL ROD

POLISHED METAL ROD

METAL ROD WITH GLASS FINIAL

BRASS ROD

METAL CAFÉ ROD

Decorative wood and metal curtain rods are available with a variety of interestingly shaped finials and may come with coordinating rings and small brackets.

COVERING A BALL FINIAL WITH FABRIC

1 *Cut a fabric square about 3 inches longer on each side than the circumference of the ball.*

2 *Install the finials.*

3 *Center the wrong side of the fabric square against the end of the finial. Smooth the fabric over the finial, gathering it at the base. Secure tightly with a rubber band, a piece of elastic, or sturdy string. Arrange the fabric evenly around the finial.*

4 *Trim the fabric so that it extends about 1 inch over the panel pocket; notch the extending fabric as needed to reduce bulk.*

5 *Tuck the extending fabric neatly inside the fabric rod pocket to conceal it.*

flat panels

Simple and speedy to sew, this basic curtain style can be attached to a rod with rings or tabs, and the panel can be lined or unlined. This project is good for beginners—calculations and stitching are easy as can be.

CALCULATING YARDAGE. Measure your window and fill in the window treatment work sheet (see pages 16–18). Flat panels do not have returns. For fullness, allow only 1½ to 2 times the finished width, rather than the usual 2½. Use the following allowances in your calculations:

LOWER HEM	8"
SIDE HEMS	6" TOTAL
TOP HEM	3"

UNLINED FLAT PANELS STEP-BY-STEP

1 Choose and prepare fabric, and join the fabric widths (see pages 21–23). Press seams open.

2 Fold and stitch lower hems (see page 24).

3 Fold and stitch side hems (see page 25).

4 On right side of fabric, measure from lower edge a distance equal to finished length. Mark with pins every 4 inches across panel.

5 Measure and mark 3-inch top hem allowance above pin-marked finished-length line. Trim ravel allowance.

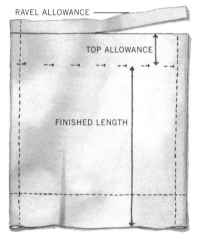

RAVEL ALLOWANCE

TOP ALLOWANCE

FINISHED LENGTH

6 Fold down top edge, wrong side in, along finished-length line; press. Remove pins. Turn raw edge in to meet pressed fold and press again. Stitch close to second fold.

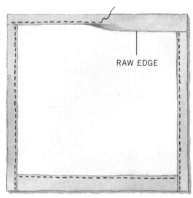

RAW EDGE

LINED FLAT PANELS STEP-BY-STEP

Use the following allowances when calculating yardage:

	FABRIC	LINING
LOWER HEM	8"	4"
SIDE HEMS	3" TOTAL	2½" TOTAL
TOP SEAM	1½"	NONE

1 Follow steps 1, 2, and 4, "Unlined flat panels," this page, for face fabric; follow steps 1 and 2 for lining. (Do not stitch side seams.)

2 Place lining on face fabric, right sides together, so lower edge of lining is 1 inch above lower edge of face fabric. Starting at leading edge, align first seams of face fabric and lining.

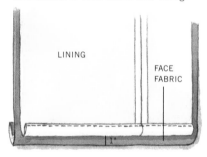

LINING

FACE FABRIC

1"

3 Trim face fabric or lining as necessary so lining is ¼ inch narrower than face fabric at each side.

4 Trim lining so upper edge meets pin-marked finished-length line on face fabric. Then, on face fabric, measure and mark 1½ inches above finished-length line. Trim ravel allowance.

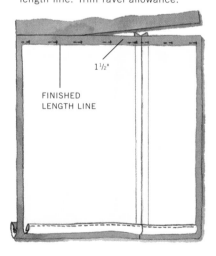

1½"

FINISHED LENGTH LINE

5 Remove lining. To face upper edge of lining so it doesn't show from front, cut a 4½-inch strip of face fabric equal in length to cut width of lining. With right sides together and raw edges aligned, pin and stitch facing to top edge of lining, making a 1½-inch seam. Press facing up (it is a continuation of the lining); then press seam allowances up.

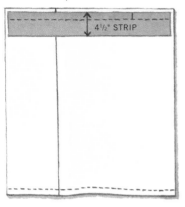

6 Place lining on face fabric, right sides together, with lower edge of lining 1 inch above lower edge of face fabric and side edges aligned (lining is slightly narrower); pin along sides. Starting at bottom of lining, stitch, making 1½-inch seams.

7 Turn panel right side out, lining side up, so an equal amount of face fabric shows at each side. With seam allowances toward center, press.

curtains on rings

Rings are a simple way to hang a curtain panel without gathering or pleating. To determine how many rings you'll need, divide width of each panel by 5 inches (a trial space size) to find approximate number of spaces needed; round off to nearest whole number. Divide width by whole number of spaces for actual space size. To determine number of rings or hooks needed, add 1 to number of spaces.

At each end of panel, sew or clip a ring to top edge; or insert point of drapery hook just below lower row of stitching. Space additional rings or hooks according to your calculations.

eyelet heading

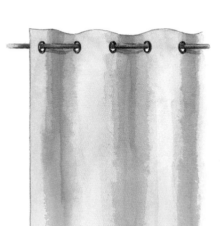

Large eyelets, also called grommets, are an alternative to rings and work well for curtains that are not pulled back often. Using a tool provided by the manufacturer, install the eyelets no more than 8 inches apart; position the end ones 1½ inches in from the finished side edges.

To attach the curtain, you can thread the rod through the eyelets as shown above. Or you can thread a decorative cord, a rope, or a heavy-weight ribbon alternately through the eyelets and around the rod, securing the cord to the rod at each end.

tab curtains

A tailored alternative to curtains with rings, tab curtains have a distinctly crisp, casual look.

TABS INSERTED IN LINED CURTAINS STEP-BY-STEP

1 Follow steps 1–6, "Lined flat panels," pages 38–39; do not sew the top edges together.

2 For tabs, drape a strip of fabric over rod. Pin and measure desired length; add 3 inches for two 1½-inch seam allowances to arrive at cut length (10 inches minimum). Finished width of tabs can vary (1½ to 2 inches is standard); add 1 inch for two ½-inch seam allowances to arrive at cut width.

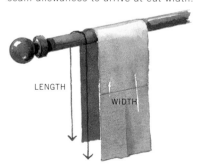

3 To figure number of spaces, subtract finished width of one tab from finished width of panel; divide by 6 inches (a trial space size) and round up to next whole number for number of spaces. (For example, for a 60-inch-wide finished panel with 2-inch-wide finished tabs, subtract 2 from 60 to get 58; divide by 6. Round result, 9.67, up to 10.)

To get actual space size, again subtract finished tab width from finished panel width and divide by number of spaces. (In example, divide 58 by 10 for a space size of 5.8, or 5¾ inches.)

Mark off spaces at top edge of face fabric, right side up, starting with a mark at half a tab width from each end of panel.

Number of tabs needed is equal to number of spaces plus 1.

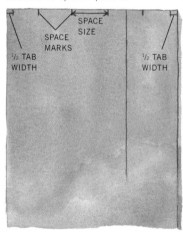

4 Cut lengthwise strips of fabric long enough so you can cut several tabs from each strip (this is easier and faster than stitching and turning each tab individually). Fold each strip in half lengthwise, right side in, and stitch the long edges together, making a ½-inch seam. Turn right side out and press so seam is at center. Cut tabs until you have the required number. Fold each tab in half crosswise, seam on the inside.

5 Turn curtain wrong side out. Sandwich folded tabs, raw edges even with top edges of curtain and folds pointing down, between face fabric and facing, placing a tab against each side fold and centering remaining tabs over space marks. Sew top raw edges together through all thicknesses.

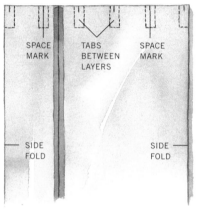

6 Turn curtain right side out and press. For added stability, topstitch 1¼ inches from top edge through all layers.

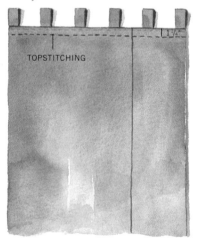

TABS TOPSTITCHED TO UNLINED CURTAINS STEP-BY-STEP

1 To determine the tab length, follow steps 2–3, "Tabs inserted in lined curtains," page 40, adding 3 inches total to cut length of each tab.

2 To make tabs, follow step 4, "Tabs inserted in lined curtains," page 40, but do not fold tabs in half. Turn each tab wrong side out; stitch across one end. Turn right side out and press.

3 Follow steps 1–5, "Unlined flat panels," page 38.

4 Follow step 6, "Unlined flat panels," page 38. Before topstitching, insert unfinished ends of tabs 1/2 inch under hem turndown, aligning a tab with each side edge and centering remaining tabs over space marks.

Topstitch close to the second fold.

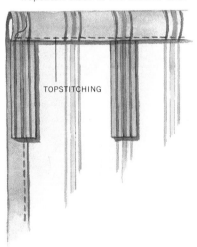

TOPSTITCHING

5 Bring tabs to the front of the curtain. Align finished ends 1 1/2 inches below top of curtain. Topstitch a square on each tab, then add an X or other decorative stitch pattern.

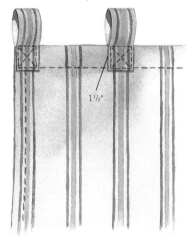

1 1/2"

button tabs

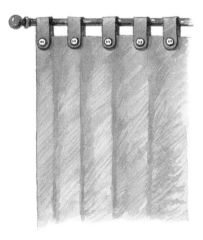

For a tailored look, button one end of the tab to the front of the curtain. Plan the tab length in the usual way, but curve or point the front end, adding an overlap allowance equal to somewhat more than the button diameter.

Follow instructions for attaching topstitched tabs to unlined curtains. Make a buttonhole in the finished end of each tab. Sew a button to the curtain opposite each folded-down tab.

knotted and bow-tied tabs

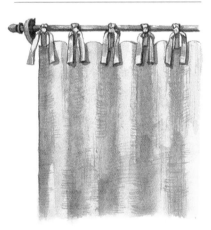

For tabs that are tied in knots or bows, experiment with strips of fabric tied and placed over the rod or pole, as in step 2, "Tabs inserted in lined curtains," page 40, to determine the length and width you'll need.

Instead of one looped tab, you'll need pairs of tabs. Turn each tab wrong side out and stitch across one end. Turn right side out and press. For tabs that are tied in bows in front, make the back tabs longer than the front tabs.

Stitch pairs of tabs to the top edge, following instructions for either lined or unlined curtain tab insertion.

decorative edgings

Custom finishes, such as ruffles and banding, lend sophistication and style to ordinary window treatments. Ruffles usually decorate rod-pocket curtains; fabric bands can be added to flat panels or rod-pocket curtains.

RUFFLES

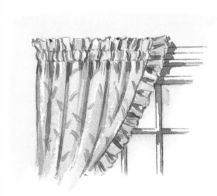

Ruffles can add texture and interest along the bottom of a shaped valance or down a curtain's leading edge.

MEASURING AND CALCULATING YARDAGE. *Cutting ruffle strips on the crosswise grain is the most economical use of the fabric. Some patterns call for lengthwise strips. When you're working with a plaid or stripe fabric, consider bias-cut ruffles.*

1 *Taking into account scale of treatment and fabric, determine finished width of ruffle (most are 1½ to 3 inches wide). For a single-thickness hemmed ruffle, add 1 inch (½ inch for seam allowance and ½ inch for a narrow hem) to finished width to arrive at cut width. For a folded ruffle, a more common style, double the finished width and add 1 inch for two ½-inch seam allowances.*

2 *Measure edges for ruffle and then multiply by 2 or 2½ for total strip length. Divide total strip length by usable fabric width and round up to nearest whole number to determine the number of crosswise strips needed.*

3 *Multiply cut width of each strip by number of strips and divide by 36 inches for yards needed.*

MAKING RUFFLES. *You'll need to piece fabric strips to make ruffles.*

1 *Cut strips as needed. To join, arrange strips, right sides together, at a right angle and seam on bias. Trim seam allowance; press open.*

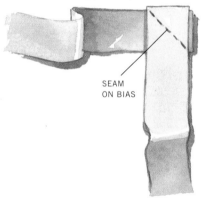

SEAM ON BIAS

2 *For a hemmed ruffle, fold each short edge in ½ inch, wrong side in, and press; turn raw edge in to meet pressed fold and press again. Machine-stitch ends. Repeat along one long edge.*

For a folded ruffle, fold pieced strip in half lengthwise, right side in, and stitch across ends, making ¼-inch seams. Turn right side out and press in half lengthwise.

3 *Zigzag (use wide stitch) over a cord (buttonhole twist or crochet cotton) about ⅜ inch from raw edge. Backstitch over cord at one end to secure.*

ATTACHING RUFFLES. *To attach a single-thickness ruffle or a folded ruffle to to the side edges of an unlined curtain, first remove the side hem allowances, leaving ½-inch seam allowances on each side. After making lower hem, serge the ruffle and panel together.*

To attach a single-thickness ruffle or a folded ruffle to a lined curtain, trim the face fabric side hem allowances even with edge of lining.

1 *Follow steps 1–2 and 4–5, "Unlined rod-pocket curtains," page 46, to make lower hems, measure and mark finished-length line, and trim top edge of face fabric and lining.*

2 *Divide ruffle strip and edge to be ruffled into fourths, marking off each section with a pin. (Note that ruffle extends from the finished lower edge to the finished-length line at the top.)*

3 *With raw edges on right sides aligned, match pins on ruffle and curtain edge; pin. Gather ruffle strip to fit edge. Baste just inside zigzag line.*

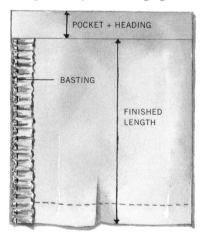

POCKET + HEADING

BASTING

FINISHED LENGTH

4 Pin lining to face fabric, right sides together, sandwiching ruffle between layers. Using basting as guide, stitch a ½-inch seam. Remove gathering cord. Serge the seams together. Turn panel right sides out and press edges.

5 Press face fabric seam allowance on each side of pocket/heading allowance.

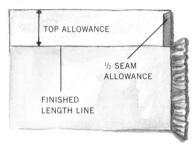

6 Fold pocket/heading on finished-length line and press. Turn raw edge in to meet pressed fold and press again. Stitch pocket and heading, if used, as instructed in step 6, "Unlined rod-pocket curtains," page 46, stopping stitching at ruffle.

CONTRAST BANDING

On curtains or draperies (lined treatments only), bands of fabric on or near leading edges create a visual border. You have two options: on-the-edge banding or set-in banding. Banding is attached after the lower hems are stitched but before the lining goes in.

For unlined treatments, on-the-edge binding finishes both sides of a curtain with clean miters at the corners. Both lower hems and side hems are removed to allow for these contrasting extensions.

ON-THE-EDGE BANDING. This simple trimming goes along the leading edge and wraps around to the wrong side.

1 Cut a contrast strip two times desired finished width as seen from front plus 3½ inches. Cut length of band is equal to distance from top cut edge of face fabric to 2 inches beyond lower hem fold.

2 Press and stitch lower hems on face fabric and lining. With right sides together and raw edges aligned at top and sides, stitch band to edge of face fabric, making a seam equal to width of finished band. Stitch to end of band.

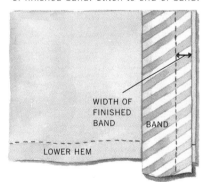

3 Turn panel wrong side up, open up band, and press seam allowances toward band. Fold band against and over raw edges and press.

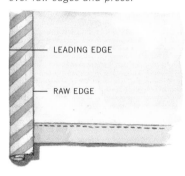

4 Flip panel right side up and open up band. Pin lining to band, right sides together and raw edges aligned, positioning lower edge of lining 1 inch above lower edge of face fabric. Stitch a 1½-inch seam.

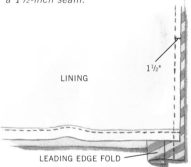

5 Press seam allowance toward band. (On back of panel, 1½ inches of band will show.)

6 At lower edge, open lining, turn up band even with lower hem, and hand-stitch to hem.

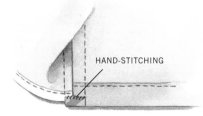

On-the-edge banding with mitered corner: *This banding trims the leading edge and the hem of the panel.*

1 *Determine finished width of border. Subtract lower hem and side hem allowances plus finished band width, and then add seam allowances for cut panel size.*

Cut a contrast strip twice the width of finished binding plus 1 inch. Cut length of band long enough to border all curtain edges plus several inches.

2 *Press band in half lengthwise, wrong side in. Press seam allowances to the wrong side on both long edges. Open out one folded seam allowance and pin to edge of curtain, right sides together. Starting at center of one side, stitch along pressed foldline, stopping just before corner at point where seamlines intersect; backtack.*

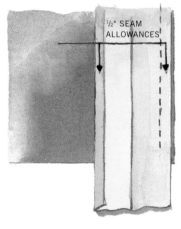

3 *Keep outer seam allowance folded; fold binding diagonally, wrong side in. Measure from binding's center fold twice width of finished binding and mark with a pin.*

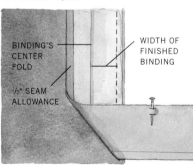

4 *Fold binding back along pin mark, right side in, and pin raw edge of binding to bottom edge of curtain. Draw a diagonal line across binding from stitched seamline to crosswise foldline. Continue down to point where adjoining seams intersect. The two diagonal lines should form a right angle. Stitch along the marked line through binding only. Trim excess binding fabric.*

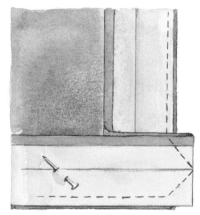

5 *Continue to stitch binding along adjoining edges, starting each side at point where seams intersect. Miter all corners. Turn binding to wrong side and slipstitch folded edge to seamline.*

SET-IN BANDING. *This trimming is applied 1½ inches from the edge of the face fabric, allowing the face fabric to show at the edge.*

Banding that ends at the lower edge of the fabric:

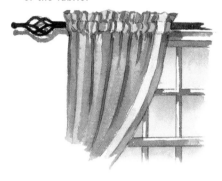

1 *Cut a contrast strip the finished width plus 1 inch. Cut length is equal to the cut length of the face fabric.*

2 *Fold ½ inch to wrong side of one long edge; press. Measuring finished width from fold, press under seam allowance on other long edge.*

3 *Mark a line on face fabric 4½ inches from leading edge. With raw edges aligned at top and bottom, pin leading edge of band to right side of face fabric. Topstitch, stitching in same direction on each edge.*

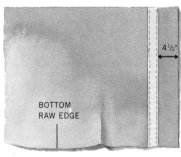

BOTTOM RAW EDGE

4½"

4 *Make lower hems on face fabric. Attach lining as directed in project.*

Mitered banding that continues above the panel hem:

1 *Determine finished width of trim and how far from edge to place it. (A 2-inch-wide band set 1½ inches from leading edge and 4¼ inches from bottom—so trim does not interfere with hem stitching—is typical.)*

Follow steps 1–2, "Set-in banding," this page, to cut, fold, and press contrast strip.

2 *Make lower hems on face fabric and lining. Mark a line on face fabric 4½ inches from leading edge and 4¼ inches from lower hem. Pin band to face fabric so leading edge of band aligns with marked line.*

Topstitch inner edge of band, stopping a distance equal to the finished width of the band from the adjacent marked line.

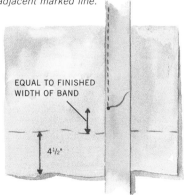

EQUAL TO FINISHED WIDTH OF BAND

4½"

3 *Fold the band back on itself along the adjacent marked line. Draw a diagonal line from the corner to the last stitch on the inner edge; stitch along the diagonal line. Trim excess band along the seamline.*

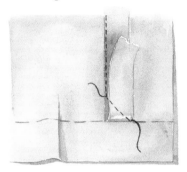

4 *Continue sewing the inner edge of the band, pivoting at each corner.*

5 *Topstitch the leading edge of the band, pivoting at each corner; press.*

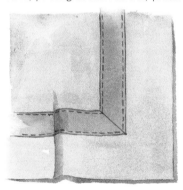

rod-pocket curtains

Soft and traditional, this basic curtain style can be shirred on a flat or round rod or pole of any size. You can make them with or without a heading; the instructions cover both. A heading above the pocket forms an instant ruffle as the rod is inserted.

A simple trick for softening the top of a rod-pocket curtain is to sew a heading twice as wide as you would like it to appear at the window. Then, after slipping the rod or pole through the pocket, pouf the heading by separating the two thicknesses.

ROD-POCKET CHART. The rod pocket must be large enough to accommodate the rod or pole comfortably and to allow the curtain to gather on the rod. Following are rod-pocket sizes for standard rods; use the appropriate pocket size when calculating yardage.

ROD TYPE	ROD DIAMETER	POCKET SIZE
SASH OR FLAT	UP TO $3/4$"	$1\frac{1}{2}$"
ROUND	UP TO 1"	$2\frac{1}{4}$"
	UP TO $1\frac{1}{2}$"	$3\frac{1}{4}$"
	UP TO 2"	$4\frac{1}{4}$"
	UP TO 3"	$5\frac{1}{2}$"
WIDE	$2\frac{1}{2}$"	$3\frac{1}{2}$"
	$4\frac{1}{2}$"	$5\frac{1}{2}$"

CALCULATING YARDAGE. Measure your window and fill in the window treatment work sheet (see pages 16–18). For most curtains, a fullness of $2\frac{1}{2}$ times the finished width is best. If your fabric is sheer, multiply finished width by 3. You'll need extra fabric for the tiebacks (see pages 52–55).

Use the following allowances in your calculations:

LOWER HEMS	8"
SIDE HEMS	6" TOTAL
TOP	2 × POCKET + 2 × HEADING (IF USED)

UNLINED ROD-POCKET CURTAINS STEP-BY-STEP

1 Choose and prepare fabric, and join the fabric widths (see pages 21–23). Press seams open.

2 Fold and stitch lower hems (see page 24).

3 Fold and stitch side hems (see page 25).

4 On right side of fabric, measure from lower edge a distance equal to finished length. Mark with pins every 4 inches across panel.

5 Measure and mark proper top allowance (2 times pocket plus 2 times heading, if used) above finished-length line. Trim ravel allowance.

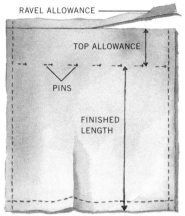

6 Fold down top edge, wrong side in, along finished-length line; press. Remove pins. Turn raw edge in to meet pressed fold and press again. Stitch close to second fold. For heading, if used, stitch again from top fold a distance equal to heading depth; press.

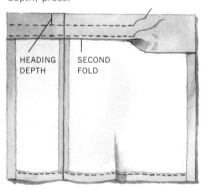

7 Slip rod through pocket between back two layers of fabric, gathering fabric evenly.

LINED ROD-POCKET CURTAIN STEP-BY-STEP

Use the following allowances in your calculations for the lining:

LOWER HEMS	4"
SIDE HEMS	NONE
TOP	NONE

1 Follow steps 1–2, 4–5, "Unlined rod-pocket curtains," page 46.

2 Cut lining 3 inches longer than the finished length of curtain and 6 inches narrower than cut width of curtain. Seam and press widths, aligning curtain and lining seams.

3 Turn, press, and stitch 2-inch double lower hem on the lining. With right sides together, pin lining to face fabric so edges are aligned at one side and lower hemmed edge of lining is 1 inch above lower hemmed edge of curtain. Lining ends at top fold line. Stitch 1½-inch-wide seam. Repeat on other side and press seam allowances toward face fabric.

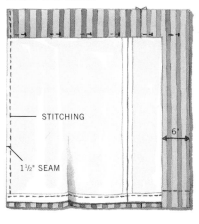

4 To complete the curtain, follow steps 5–7, "Unlined rod-pocket curtains," page 46.

rod sleeve

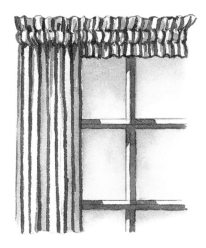

When rod-pocket curtains don't meet in the center but just hang at the sides of the window, a simple sleeve that fits on the rod between the panels visually bridges the gap and completes the treatment.

If the panels on either side have a heading, give the rod sleeve the same heading. For a custom look, add another heading below the rod pocket.

CALCULATING YARDAGE. The following method of determining yardage gives even fullness across the rod.

1 Multiply rod length by 2½ and subtract finished width (flat measurement) of side panels. Divide remainder by usable fabric width and round to the nearest whole number to arrive at number of widths needed for sleeve.

2 The cut length (up-and-down measurement) is equal to 2 times rod pocket plus 2 times heading depth for each heading, if used, plus 1 inch. For patterned fabric, calculate repeat cut length (see page 20). Try to match the pattern horizontally on sleeve and curtain pockets.

3 Multiply cut length or repeat cut length by number of widths and divide by 36 inches for yards needed.

ROD SLEEVE STEP-BY-STEP

1 Join fabric widths as described on page 23. Press seams open.

2 Make a ½-inch hem on each end. Fold fabric in half lengthwise, right side in. Pin and stitch long edges together, making a ½-inch seam. Turn right side out. Center seam at back and press.

3 For a single heading, if used, stitch from top fold a distance equal to heading depth; for a double heading, if used, stitch upper and lower edges a distance equal to heading depth.

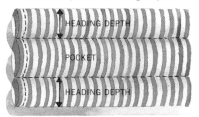

4 Slip rod through pocket, gathering fabric evenly.

sash curtain

Gathered and stretched on two rods, an unlined sash curtain is a good choice for a casement window or a French door—the lower rod keeps the curtain in place when the window or door is opened or closed. A sash curtain can be made either with or without headings.

CALCULATING YARDAGE. Measure your window and fill in the window treatment work sheet (see pages 16–18). For most sash curtains, a fullness of 2½ times the finished width is best. If you are using a sheer fabric, multiply the finished width by 3.

Use the following allowances in your calculations. Remember that you need a pocket (and a heading, if used) at both top and bottom. Refer to the top chart on page 46 for pocket size.

TOP AND BOTTOM	2 × POCKET + 2 × HEADING (IF USED)
SIDE HEMS	6" TOTAL

SASH CURTAIN STEP-BY-STEP

1 Choose and prepare fabric. Join the fabric widths and finish seams (see pages 21–24).

2 Fold and stitch side hems (see page 25).

3 Turn up lower edge, wrong side in, a distance equal to bottom allowance; press. Turn raw edge in to meet pressed fold and press again. Stitch as you did side hems; press. For the bottom heading, if used, stitch from the lower fold a distance equal to the heading depth.

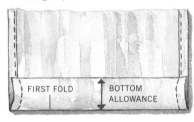

FIRST FOLD BOTTOM ALLOWANCE

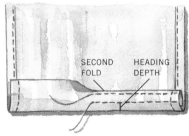

SECOND FOLD HEADING DEPTH

4 On right side of face fabric, measure from lower edge a distance equal to finished length and mark with pins every 4 inches across panel.

5 Measure and mark proper top allowances (2 times pocket plus 2 times heading, if used) above the pin-marked finished-length line. Trim the ravel allowance.

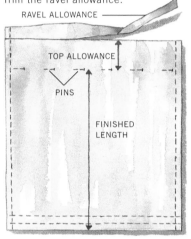

RAVEL ALLOWANCE

TOP ALLOWANCE

PINS

FINISHED LENGTH

6 Fold down top edge, wrong side in, along finished-length line; press. Remove pins. Turn raw edge in to meet pressed fold and press again. For heading, if used, stitch again from top fold a distance equal to heading depth.

7 Slip rods through pockets between back two layers of fabric, gathering fabric evenly. Install top rod, and then bottom rod so curtain is taut.

hourglass curtain

A cousin to the sash curtain, the hourglass style evokes a range of decorating moods depending on the fabric chosen.

Because of the tension on the curtain, the curtain must be at least a third longer than the rod length. (If, for example, your rod is 24 inches, the curtain must be 32 inches or longer.) Any curtain closer to square than this won't stay in the hourglass configuration.

CALCULATING YARDAGE. Measure your window and fill in the window treatment work sheet (see pages 16–18). For most hourglass curtains, a fullness of 2¹/₂ times the finished width is best. If you are using a sheer fabric, multiply the finished width by 3.

Use the following allowances in your calculations. Remember that you need a pocket (and a heading, if used) at both top and bottom. Allow additional fabric for a tieback and, if desired, a rosette. Refer to the top chart on page 46 for pocket size.

TOP AND BOTTOM	2 × POCKET + 2 × HEADING (IF USED)
SIDE HEMS	6" TOTAL
STRETCH ALLOWANCE	4"

HOURGLASS CURTAIN STEP-BY-STEP

1 Choose and prepare fabric. Join fabric widths and finish the seams (see pages 21–24).

2 Fold and stitch side hems (see page 25).

3 Fold fabric panel in half crosswise, lining up side seams, and press fold at center. Fold panel lengthwise and press again at center. Mark center point where folds intersect with a safety pin or use a fabric marker.

4 Measure from center point toward top a distance equal to half the finished length; measure and mark the same distance from center point toward the bottom. Mark with pins every 4 inches across panel.

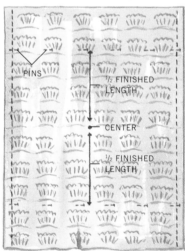

5 At side hems, add 2 inches to pinned lines at both top and bottom and mark these points. (Finished length of panel is now 4 inches more at edges than at center.) At top and bottom, draw a gentle curve from marks at side edges to center to mark new finished-length line.

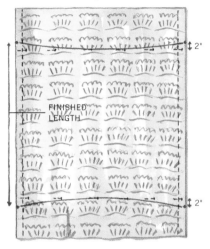

6 Using first curve as a reference, draw another curve at top and bottom a distance equal to top and bottom allowance (2 times pocket plus 2 times heading, if used). Cut on second curved lines; remove pins.

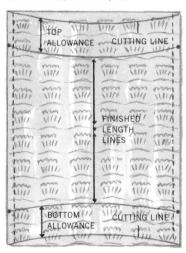

7 Fold down top edge, wrong side in, along curved finished-length line; press. Turn raw edge in to meet pressed fold and press again. Stitch close to second fold. For heading, if used, stitch again from top fold a distance equal to heading depth. Repeat for lower pocket.

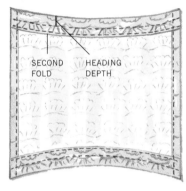

8 Slip sash rods into rod pockets between back two layers of fabric, gathering fabric evenly. Mount curtain, installing top rod first and then bottom rod so curtain is taut in center.

9 To determine size of tieback, pull panel into hourglass shape at center and tie with string or scrap fabric (make sure side hems are straight and ends of rods are covered). Add 2 inches for overlap to arrive at finished length of tieback and add 1 inch for seam allowances. The finished width should be between 2 and 3 inches; double that figure and add 1 inch for seam allowances.

10 To make tieback, see pages 52–53. To make rosette or other embellishment, see pages 126–127.

sunburst curtain

A sunburst curtain is actually a type of sash curtain, except the lower hem is gathered and pulled through a ring to fill a fan-shaped window. Choose a lightweight or sheer fabric for this style, and when possible, railroad the fabric to avoid seams.

This curtain works best if the window's radius is 36 inches or less; on a window larger than that, you'll have too much fabric at the center. Also, because a sunburst curtain relies on equal tension from the center out to the curve, you'll get the best results on half-circle windows. Don't use a sunburst curtain on an elliptical window if the difference between the window's height and the radius at the base is greater than 6 inches.

Hang the curtain on a flexible clear rod supported with brackets. You'll also need a wood drapery ring with an eyelet to form the rosette and a cup hook to secure the ring.

CALCULATING YARDAGE. Refer to the drawing below as you measure.

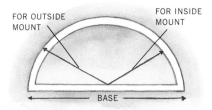

FOR OUTSIDE MOUNT
FOR INSIDE MOUNT
BASE

1 For number of fabric widths, measure window's finished width, or curve, and multiply by 2 for fullness; add 6 inches for side hems. For fabric that runs vertically, divide figure by usable fabric width. If railroading fabric, divide figure by 36 inches to determine the yards needed.

2 To find finished length, divide base of window by 2 and add 3 inches to allow for rosette; for an outside mount, add coverage beyond opening. For top allowance on an inside or outside mount, add 5 inches total for a 1½-inch pocket and a 1-inch heading (a heading is recommended even on an inside mount to ensure a snug fit). Add 6 inches for hem at base.

3 For fabric that runs vertically, multiply cut length by number of widths and divide by 36 inches for yards needed.

SUNBURST CURTAIN STEP-BY-STEP

1 Choose and prepare fabric. Join the fabric widths and finish the seams (see pages 21–24).

2 Fold and stitch side hems (see page 25).

3 Turn up lower hem 6 inches, wrong side in, and press. Turn raw edge in to meet pressed fold and press again. Stitch close to second fold.

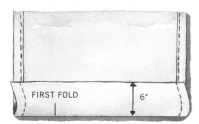

FIRST FOLD   6"

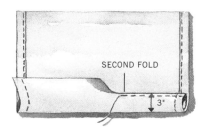

SECOND FOLD   3"

4 On right side of fabric, measure from lower hem a distance equal to finished length plus 3 inches for finished-length line; mark with pins every 4 inches across panel. Measure and mark 5 inches beyond pin-marked line. Trim ravel allowance.

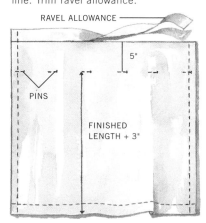

RAVEL ALLOWANCE
5"
PINS
FINISHED LENGTH + 3"

5 Fold top, wrong side in, on finished-length line; press. Remove pins. Turn raw edge in to meet pressed fold and press again. Stitch close to second fold. For heading, stitch again 1 inch from top fold.

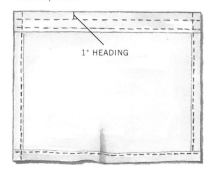

1" HEADING

6 Slip rod through pocket, adjusting gathers evenly, and mount. To make rosette, gather lower hem and pull through ring.

7 For an outside mount, screw in a cup hook below center point of window. Turn hook sideways, slip eyelet over, and turn hook down. For an inside mount, screw hook into sill; slip eyelet over hook.

curtain and drapery tiebacks

Tiebacks hold treatments back from the window, shaping the treatment and letting in light. For a pair of tiebacks, you will need fabric, four ½-inch-diameter rings, and a pair of concealed tieback holders (or two cup hooks).

TAILORED TIEBACKS

For tailored tiebacks, you'll need two strips of heavy fusible interfacing.

1 To determine the finished size, wrap a tape measure gently around the curtain panel, bring the tape together, and swing it to the molding or wall where you'll attach a hook. A general rule of thumb is that a tailored tieback is half the rod length plus 4 inches.

2 Install concealed tieback holders into the wall or window trim or screw in cup hooks.

3 To determine the cut size, add 1 inch to the finished length; double the finished width and add 1 inch. For each tieback, cut one strip of fabric on the lengthwise grain and one strip of heavy fusible interfacing ½ inch smaller all around.

4 Center fusible interfacing on wrong side of tieback and fuse in place. Press short ends ½ inch to wrong side.

5 Fold strip in half lengthwise, right side in. Stitch long edges together, making a ½-inch seam.

6 Turn tieback right side out so lengthwise seam is face up and centered. Press. Turn pressed ends inside and slipstitch closed.

7 Leave ends square or press corners diagonally to inside to form a point and slipstitch in place. Hand-sew a ring to each end.

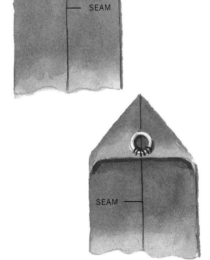

SHAPED TIEBACKS

Shaped tiebacks are a little more graceful than tailored tiebacks and fit the contour of the curtain fabric as it falls into place.

1 To make a pattern, cut a strip of medium-weight paper 4 to 6 inches wide and slightly longer than the tieback will be. Pin the paper around the curtain panel. Draw a curved shape and trim the paper, experimenting until you get the effect you want.

2 For each tieback, use the paper pattern to cut two pieces from fabric, adding a ½-inch seam allowance all around. Cut one piece from fusible interfacing without adding seam allowance. Fuse the interfacing to the wrong side of one fabric piece.

3 Place both pieces right sides together, and stitch all around with a ½-inch seam allowance. Leave an opening on one long edge for turning. Trim seams and clip curves.

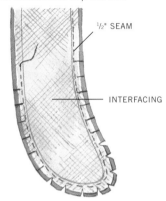

½" SEAM

INTERFACING

4 Turn tieback right side out and press. Slipstitch the opening closed. Hand-sew rings to each end at least ¼ inch from the edge.

SHIRRED TIEBACKS

In addition to face fabric, you'll need lining, heavy fusible interfacing, and contrast welt.

1 Follow steps 1–2, "Tailored tiebacks," (see page 52).

2 To determine the cut size, multiply finished length by 2 and add 2 inches; add 1 inch to finished width. For each tieback, cut one strip of fabric on lengthwise grain. For lining, add 2 inches to finished length and 1 inch to finished width; cut one lining strip. Cut one strip of fusible interfacing equal to finished length and width. Fuse to the wrong side of the lining.

3 To shirr the fabric strip, zigzag over a cord (buttonhole twist or crochet cotton) down each long edge. Gather each edge to the finished length plus 2 inches. With raw edges aligned, baste welt to right side of tieback. Remove the welt cord in the seam allowances at each end to reduce bulk.

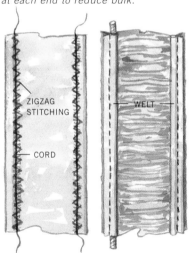

ZIGZAG STITCHING

WELT

CORD

4 Pin lining to tieback, right sides together, and stitch close to welt, using previous stitching as a guide. Turn right side out.

5 Turn under 1 inch on each open end and slipstitch closed. Hand-sew rings to wrong side of tiebacks.

TIED SASH

A long band of fabric wrapped around the curtain and tied in a bow or knot is a simple and often very effective tieback. Your choice of fabric and the way you tie it makes a sash elegant, casual, or whimsical.

To determine the sash length, tie a scarf or ribbon around the curtain and make a bow; then measure the length of the scarf or ribbon.

Sew a ring to the middle of the sash. Place the ring over the hook on the window trim, and wrap and tie the sash around the curtain.

JUMBO WELT TIEBACKS

Plump cord ³/₄ inch or more in diameter gives jumbo welt tiebacks their soft, oversize look. Choose a cord size appropriate to the scale of the treatment. With this method, you'll have leftover cord.

1 For two tiebacks, cut a length of cord equal to four times the finished length of one tieback plus 4 inches. Cut a strip of fabric equal to twice the finished length of one tieback plus 2 inches, and 1 inch wider than the cord circumference. If piecing is necessary, try to position seam at the midpoint.

2 Starting at midpoint of cord, wrap strip of fabric around cord, right side in, aligning raw edges. Using a zipper foot, stitch down long edge of fabric close to cord (don't crowd cord). Hand-stitch securely across the starting point.

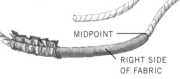

MIDPOINT

HAND-STITCHING

3 Pull end of cord free from casing and hold securely. At starting point, slide fabric over itself toward uncovered cord until fabric tube is right side out.

MIDPOINT

RIGHT SIDE OF FABRIC

Cut off excess cord at starting point. Cut fabric-covered portion of cord at midpoint for two tiebacks.

4 To finish ends, trim out ¹/₂ inch of cord; turn casing to inside and slipstitch closed. Sew rings to the ends.

KNOTTED WELT TIEBACKS

To determine finished length of one tieback, tie a decorative knot in a length of cord and tie back a panel, adjusting length and height until effect is pleasing. Mark desired finished length on cord; remove, untie, and measure.

Make two jumbo welt tiebacks to this length. Make a decorative knot near center before installing tieback.

SHIRRED WELT TIEBACKS

For each tieback, cut a fabric strip 2 times the tieback length and 2 inches wider than the circumference of the cord. Follow the method for turning jumbo welt tiebacks to encase the cord, gathering the fabric as the tube is turned. Finish ends; attach rings.

BRAIDED WELT TIEBACKS

Cut cording 9 times the finished length of tieback plus 4 inches. Cut fabric 4½ times the length of tieback. For one tieback, cut cord 9 times the tieback length plus 4 inches. Cut fabric 4½ times the length of tieback. Follow the method for turning jumbo welt tiebacks to encase the cord. Cut cord at starting point. Cut covered cord into three equal sections.

To make a braid with three different fabrics, make three separate cords, each one twice the finished length plus 2 inches.

Turn ends of all three pieces to the inside; slipstitch. Overlap the three tubes slightly at one end. Hand-sew tubes together and braid. Cut other ends of tubes when braid reaches desired tieback length; slipstitch to finish. Attach rings.

TIEBACK HARDWARE

Decorative hardware and accessories are sometimes used instead of fabric tiebacks to secure draped panels. Holdbacks are available in a wide variety of styles and finishes. They can match the drapery rod style or be design elements on their own. From metal to plastic to iron, tieback holders with projection arms or stems hold fabric back casually. Hook style holdbacks hold the fabric more securely.

Fabric tiebacks can be attached to concealed tieback holders, which prevent the drapery from being crushed. Cup hooks and 1¼-inch tieback hooks hold fabric tiebacks at the sides of windows. Tieback rings in plastic or metal are sewn to the back of the tieback.

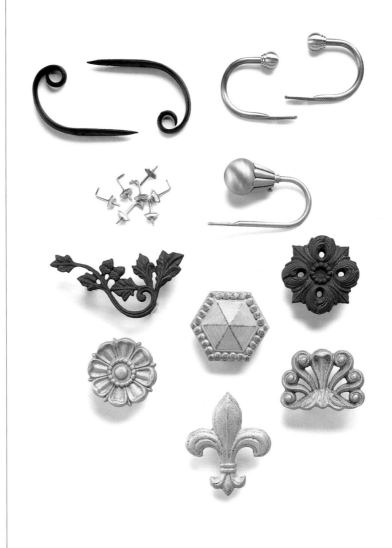

draperies

ABOVE: Bright pinch-pleated draperies form a colorful frame for a swagged Roman shade that can be adjusted for light and privacy. Magenta buttons punctuate the drapery pleats and pick up the color of the trim on the shade.

RIGHT: Pleated draperies, mounted on two separate rods, create a layered effect in contrasting colored silk fabric. Draw one pair or both, or leave them open to feature the wood blinds.

LEFT: Classic pinched-pleated draperies in a luxurious heavy silk fabric are drawn back by a strategically placed table to create maximum visibility through an important window.

BELOW: Pinch-pleated draperies in a dark, rich cotton print fall gracefully from ceiling-mounted rods to the floor to become a major design element in this formal living space.

how to make draperies

What was once the mainstay of window fashions—the pinch-pleated drapery—has evolved into a collection of appealing pleated styles. Classic pinch pleats and four variations are offered here. Once you decide on a style, look at your hardware options to select an appropriate rod.

drapery hardware

Rods and accessories (shown below and opposite) range from conventional traverse rods to decorative rods with interesting finishes and flourishes.

Home improvement centers, department stores, and large fabric stores carry hardware made by a handful of manufacturers. Investigate mail-order sources or consult a professional decorator to see a myriad of styles, just right for your treatment style and fabric.

RODS AND BRACKETS

Standard for draperies is the traverse rod, which allows you to open and close the panels by pulling a cord that moves small slides along a track.

An adjustable *conventional traverse rod* is designed to be concealed when the treatment is closed. The first two drapery hooks on the leading edge of each panel fit into a master slide; the two master slides overlap at the center of the rod.

For sliding glass doors and corner windows, use a one-way draw rod. On a bay window, try placing a one-way rod at each side and a two-way rod at the center.

Decorative traverse rods, which range in style from contemporary to traditional, are exposed whether the drapery is open or closed. Most of these rods come with half-round ring-slide combinations and with finials that attach to the ends.

End brackets can be plain or decorative. Plain ones are adjustable and placed at the ends of a conventional traverse rod, hidden from view by the draperies. Most decorative brackets are adjustable and visible; they support the rod from underneath.

Support brackets, also adjustable, ease some of the strain on long drapery rods. As a rule, you'll need one for every 40 inches of rod length.

NOTIONS AND ACCESSORIES

You'll find these items in the notions section of fabric and decorating stores.

Four-inch-wide *crinoline* (sometimes called buckram) stiffens the headings on pleated draperies. Crinoline comes in woven and nonwoven types.

Drapery hooks, available 1 and 1¼ inches long, are designed to sit in the slides of a traverse rod without shifting under the weight of the fabric. The standard 1¼-inch hook is used in most professional workrooms. The smaller 1-inch hook is sometimes used in sheer and lightweight fabrics.

Drapery weights sewn into the corners of the lower hem assure that panels will hang straight.

Concealed tieback holders and *decorative holdbacks* are sometimes used with draperies. For more information, see page 55.

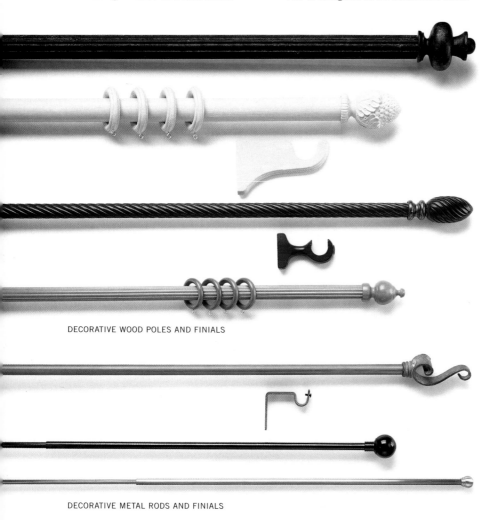

DECORATIVE WOOD POLES AND FINIALS

DECORATIVE METAL RODS AND FINIALS

Drapery rods and accessories are available in a variety of sizes, some thick enough to support lined draperies. The accompanying brackets are larger also.

hardware installation

It is always a good idea to carefully read through the manufacturer's instructions from beginning to end before beginning to install a drapery rod. Having a helper will make the installation easier.

ROD PLACEMENT

Install the rod where it will give you the coverage you determined when you measured your window and calculated the amount of fabric you needed (see pages 16–20).

Find the distance the drapery goes above the window opening. For a conventional traverse rod, set the top of the brackets at a height equal to the finished length of the window treatment, allowing for the drapery to hang $1/2$ inch above the floor.

For a decorative rod, read the manufacturer's instructions to determine the prescribed distance from the top of the drapery heading to the top screw hole on the brackets.

HOW TO MOUNT RODS

Most rods are installed in the following sequence:

1 Mount the end brackets and support brackets, if used. Use a carpenter's level to check the position of the brackets. Mark through the screw holes.

2 Mount a conventional rod by slipping it over the end brackets. For a decorative rod, arrange the rings before you tighten the brackets. For either rod, adjust the clips on any support brackets so they fit snugly over the rod.

3 Adjust the cord, mount the tension pulley, and center the master slide. Add or remove the slides or ring-slides so you have the correct number for your drapery hooks. Cut the cord only after you're sure you've allowed enough length to pull the panels shut.

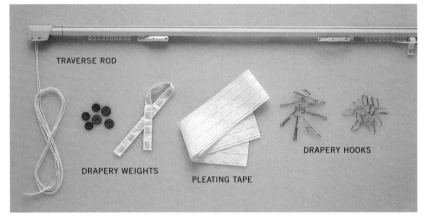

TRAVERSE ROD

DRAPERY WEIGHTS

PLEATING TAPE

DRAPERY HOOKS

Drapery notions include a traverse rod, weights available either singly or sewn into a tape, pleating tape, and drapery hooks in several sizes.

HANGING DRAPERIES

With the master slides near the center but not overlapping, start hanging one panel by inserting the first two hooks on the return edge into the holes on the bracket. Insert the remaining hooks into the slides, ending with the master slide. Repeat for the other panel.

"TRAINING" DRAPERIES

After they are hung, you can train your draperies so the pleats are crisp and the folds are uniform.

Open the panels to the stackback position. Then "comb" and smooth them with your fingers, pulling the pleated folds forward and pushing back the folds in between. Gently tie the bundle near the top and bottom with fabric strips. Leave the ties on for several days to set the folds.

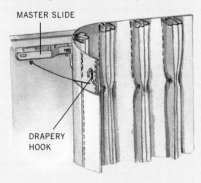

MASTER SLIDE

DRAPERY HOOK

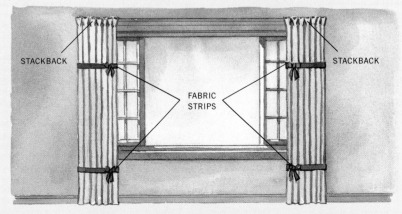

STACKBACK

STACKBACK

FABRIC STRIPS

pinch pleats

Pinch-pleated draperies and their close relatives (see the variations on pages 62–63) are versatile treatments that offer a range of looks, from classic traditional to modern. Pinch pleats are sometimes called French pleats.

The directions that follow are for a single lined panel (for an unlined version, see page 62). At each end of the panel and at every pleat, you'll need a pin-on drapery hook. For stiffener, use 4-inch-wide crinoline. If you're making two panels for a window, remember that they must be mirror images of each other.

CALCULATING YARDAGE. Measure your window and fill in the window treatment work sheet (see pages 16–18). Draperies have returns and overlaps; fullness is usually 2½ times finished width. Most draperies begin at the top of the window casing and end ½ inch above floor level.

Use the following allowances in your calculations:

	FABRIC	LINING
LOWER HEM	8"	4"
SIDE HEMS	6" TOTAL	NONE
TOP	8"	NONE

PINCH PLEATS STEP-BY-STEP

1 Choose and prepare face fabric and lining, and join the fabric widths (see pages 21–23). Press seams open.

2 Fold and stitch lower hems (see page 24).

3 On wrong side of face fabric, measure from lower hem a distance equal to finished length and mark with pins every 4 inches across panel.

4 Lay lining on face fabric, right sides together, so lower edge of lining is 1 inch above lower edge of face fabric. Starting from leading edge, align first seam of the face fabric with first seam of the lining.

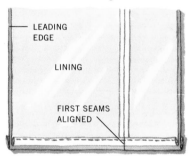

5 Trim face fabric or lining if needed so lining is 3 inches narrower than face fabric on each side.

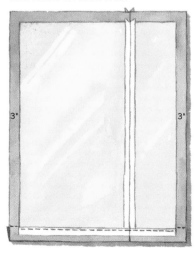

6 Trim lining so upper edge meets pin-marked finished-length line on face fabric. Then, on face fabric, measure and mark 8-inch top allowance above finished-length line. Trim ravel allowance.

7 Pin lining to face fabric, right sides together, so leading edge of lining is aligned with leading edge of face fabric (lining hem should still be 1 inch above face fabric hem). Starting at lower edge and continuing to top, stitch a 1½-inch seam.

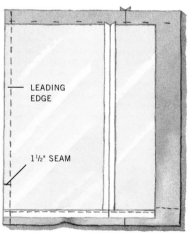

8 Separate face fabric from lining, laying both right sides down. Press seam allowances toward face fabric.

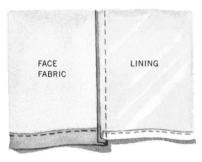

Bring lining over, wrong sides together, so 1½ inches of face fabric shows on back and seam allowance is tucked into fold; press.

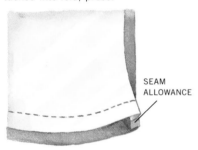

SEAM ALLOWANCE

9 With right sides together, align other side edges of lining and face fabric. Pin and stitch as in step 7. Turn panel right side out. Fold seam toward return edge as in step 8 so 1½ inches of face fabric shows at each side; press.

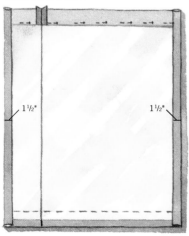

1½"   1½"

10 Fold one end of crinoline under 1 inch; place fold ¼ inch from edge of panel, aligning lower edge of crinoline with finished-length line; pin. Pin crinoline across panel to opposite side. Trim end and fold under 1 inch, positioning fold ¼ inch from edge. Remove pins from finished-length line.

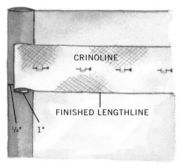

CRINOLINE

FINISHED LENGTHLINE

¼"   1"

11 Fold 4-inch allowance over crinoline, press edge, and remove pins. Fold and press again; pin in place.

SECOND FOLD

12 Stitch side of heading closed, ⅛ inch from edge; backstitch. Stitch again, 1⅜ inches from edge.

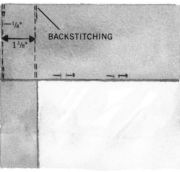

⅛"

BACKSTITCHING

1⅜"

13 *For a single-panel treatment,* subtract the width of finished drapery from the width of flat panel. *For each panel of a two-panel treatment,* subtract half of finished drapery width from width of flat panel. Record result for use in step 15.

14 Multiply number of full fabric widths in each panel by 5 and half-widths by 2 to find number of pleats per panel. Number of spaces will be one less than number of pleats.

15 To determine pleat size, divide result from step 13 by number of pleats (step 14) to arrive at fabric allowance for each pleat. Round off to nearest ¼ inch.

16 To determine amount of space between pleats, subtract return (determined previously) and 3½ inches for overlap from finished width. Divide by number of spaces between pleats (step 14) to arrive at fabric allowance for each space. Round off to nearest ¼ inch.

17 Starting at leading edge, measure in 3½ inches and pin to indicate start of first pleat (with heads of pins above top of panel). Measure and pin end of pleat and space to next pleat.

Continue across panel, marking all pleats and spaces; end with a pleat. Remaining portion should equal return measurement. Adjust pins slightly, if necessary, so last pleat ends where return begins.

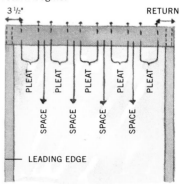

3½"   RETURN

PLEAT   PLEAT   PLEAT   PLEAT   PLEAT

SPACE   SPACE   SPACE   SPACE

LEADING EDGE

If fabric widths have been joined to make panel, readjust pins so seams fall close to edge of pleats. Don't alter size of space; make adjustments in pleats only.

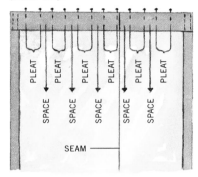

18 On wrong side of heading, bring together pins at sides of pleats. Lightly finger-press folds.

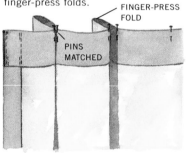

FINGER-PRESS FOLD

PINS MATCHED

Stitch pleats from bottom of crinoline to top of panel at point where pins meet; backstitch at each end. Push down on each side of each crease to form two more loops, making sure all three are even.

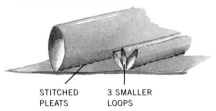

STITCHED PLEATS

3 SMALLER LOOPS

19 Drop the feed dogs on the sewing machine and zigzag a tack stitch 1/2 inch from bottom of crinoline in the center of the pleat through all layers.

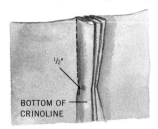

1/2"

BOTTOM OF CRINOLINE

20 To determine insertion point for drapery hooks, see chart below. Decorative rods may vary; check manufacturer's instructions.

TYPE OF ROD	INSERTION POINT	
	1" HOOK	1¼" HOOK
CONVENTIONAL (The top of the hook should be 2" from the top of the drapery.)	3"	3¼"
DECORATIVE (The top of the hook should be ½" from the top of the drapery.)	1½"	1¾"

Pin a drapery hook to the back of each pleat, to end of return, and 3/4 inch from leading edge so it pierces crinoline but not face fabric.

21 To give crinoline a pleat "memory," crease vertically at midpoint between pleats; crease forward for a conventional rod, back for a decorative rod.

UNLINED PINCH PLEATS

Draperies made from sheer and casement fabrics are unlined. Although draperies made in woven fabrics are generally lined to protect them from sun fading and to improve draping qualities, some casual drapery treatments are unlined. When making unlined pinch-pleated draperies, the same side, hem, and top allowances are used. The side hems are constructed as you would when making unlined curtains (see page 25).

goblet pleats

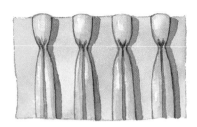

Goblet pleats are an elegant drapery heading style used only for stationary treatments. Opening and closing the draperies would crush the pleats.

1 Follow steps 1–17, "Pinch pleats," pages 60–62, to make the panels and pin-mark the pleats.

2 On wrong side of heading, bring together pins at sides of pleat. Stitch pleat from bottom of crinoline to top of panel at point where pins meet. Backstitch at each end.

3 At base of each pleat, make tucks and hand-tack just above lower edge of crinoline.

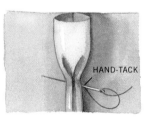

HAND-TACK

4 Open top of pleat, forming a round goblet shape. Hand-tack back of each goblet to top of panel on either side of vertical stitching.

HAND-TACKING

5 Insert drapery hooks. See step 20, "Pinch pleats," on this page.

6 Slip a roll of crinoline into each goblet to maintain shape.

butterfly pleats

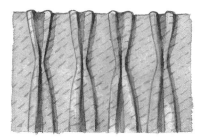

Two rather than three folds in each pleat distinguish the butterfly pleat from the basic pinch pleat.

1 Follow steps 1–17, "Pinch pleats," pages 60–62, to make the panels and pin-mark the pleats.

2 Follow step 2, "Goblet pleats," page 62, to stitch pleats.

3 Center each pleat over vertical stitching and flatten.

4 Bring folded edges together and, making sure they're even, finger-press two pleats.

FINGER-PRESSED FOLDS

5 To finish, follow steps 19–21, "Pinch pleats," page 62.

pencil pleats

Pleating tape sewn to the back of a drapery panel is used to achieve this pleat style. By pulling cords inside the tape, you can gather the heading into even, narrow, pencil-size pleats.

Select either a 3- or 4-pleat pencil-pleat drapery shirring tape and adjust the top allowance accordingly. The shirring tape substitutes for crinoline.

1 Follow steps 1–9, "Pinch pleats," pages 60–61. Allow a 1½-inch top allowance.

2 Fold down the top allowance to the wrong side and press.

3 Pin shirring tape ¼ inch down from top of panel. Pull out ½ inch of each cord at each end; turn tape under to finish ends. Stitch along top and bottom of tape and between each row of cord.

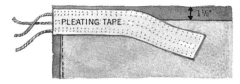

PLEATING TAPE

1½"

4 Knot ends of tape along one edge. Apply glue to knots to keep in place. Trim ends.

5 Pull other ends of cords until panel gathers up to finished width. Knot, glue, and trim pulled cord ends. Insert drapery hooks. See step 20, "Pinch pleats," page 62.

reverse pinch pleats

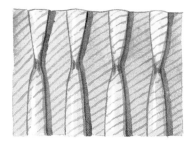

Sleek reverse pinch pleats are folded to the back.

1 Follow steps 1–17, "Pinch pleats," pages 60–62, to make the panels and pin-mark the pleats.

2 Follow step 2, "Goblet pleats," page 62, to stitch pleats.

3 Center each pleat over vertical stitching and gently flatten.

4 Roll folded edges around to touch stitching.

5 Hand-tack pleats just above lower edge of crinoline, placing stitches at back of each pleat and just catching folded edges.

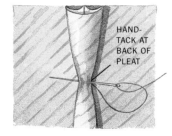

HAND-TACK AT BACK OF PLEAT

6 Insert drapery hooks. See step 20, "Pinch pleats," page 62.

The corner configuration of these windows allows for an interesting installation of balloon shades in an allover print fabric. The repeating soft poufs on the bottom edge become a focal point in the room.

ABOVE: Deep red London shades mounted on French doors match the hue on the walls in this elegant room. Each shade's scalloped bottom edge is created with a single pleat on either side of the shade.

LEFT: A tone-on-tone damask fabric gives substance to the undulating curves of this balloon shade, bringing great import to the window.

ABOVE: A striped Roman shade is a classic treatment for a tailored room, here enlivened with jaunty pennants along the ceiling. Coordinating the shade fabric with the wall covering and bed pillows unifies the room's décor.

RIGHT: Roman shades in a pretty floral print soften the angular corner windows of a breakfast room. The contrasting bands on the edges help define the windows while containing the print.

LEFT: Bold stripes make a contemporary statement for these Roman shades; crisp cotton duck fabric helps them keep their shape. Mounting the shades on the inside of the trim makes them an integral part of the windows.

BELOW: Soft-fold Roman shades, created by relaxing the fabric between the horizontal pleats, dress up plain walls and simply framed windows.

ABOVE: A cloud shade in a classic blue-and-white floral is the perfect complement to this window seat. The exaggerated width of the scallops is created by the extra-wide spacing of the rings on the back of the shade.

RIGHT: Adding a ruffle makes a cloud shade more feminine and especially fitting for a little girl's room. The fabrics used for the shade and ruffle are featured in the room's décor.

ABOVE: A fish-motif fabric showing illustrated pages from an antique natural history book makes these simple roller shades both fun and functional.

LEFT: For complete privacy and to protect furniture from the sun's penetrating rays, opaque roller shades provide the best solution. The rich color adds a strong visual element to the room and accentuates the deep window recesses.

how to make shades

Shades are as practical as they are good-looking—they control light, provide insulation, and ensure privacy. Use them alone or team them with curtains, draperies, valances, or cornices.

It's best to line Roman, balloon, and cloud shades; they hang better and the lining protects the face fabric from deterioration. And, as with other treatments, a lining provides added insulation.

inside or outside mount?

An inside-mounted shade fits between the frame on either side of the window and ends at the sill. For Roman, balloon, and cloud shades, the finished width of the shade is the width of the window opening less 1/2 inch.

An outside-mounted shade's finished width will be the width of the area you decide to cover. The lower rod comes

to the sill, with the skirt or permanent pouf, if used, covering the apron or extending below the window opening.

For an inside- or outside-mounted roller shade, the finished width of the shade will be the same as the length of the roller itself (not including the roller hardware).

hardware and notions

Roman, balloon, and cloud shades use the same basic materials; roller shades require their own hardware. For a look at shade hardware, see below.

HARDWARE FOR ROMAN, BALLOON, AND CLOUD SHADES

To make any of these shades, you'll need specialized notions from shops that carry shade and drapery supplies, as well as some general hardware store items.

Supplies for rigging the shade include 1/4- or 1/2-inch rings, Roman

shade cord or lightweight traverse cord, a shade pull, screw eyes, a small awning or shade cleat, and a 3/8-inch-diameter sash curtain rod, brass rod, or wood dowel rod 1/2 inch shorter than the finished width of your shade (use tape to hold an adjustable rod at the correct length). On extra-large shades, a pulley is mounted on the heading board to house the cords and distribute the weight of the pull system.

To mount and hang the shade, you'll need a board (typically a 1 by 2) 1/4 inch shorter than the finished width of the shade, a staple gun, and, to attach the board to the window header, either screws (for an inside mount or a flat mount on a door) or angle irons (for an outside mount).

For a cloud shade, buy shirring tape (see page 81).

ROLLER SHADE HARDWARE

If you're replacing an existing shade, you can simply cut new fabric to fit the roller you already have. Otherwise, you'll need to buy a roller (see page 83 for information on types of rollers and mountings). Wood rollers can be cut to size. Before you cut, note the difference in the ends; the pin end is the one to cut off; the blade end contains the spring mechanism that makes the shade roll up.

With pliers, remove the pin and end cap. Cut the roller with a saw, making sure you don't cut through the spring. Replace the end cap and pound in the pin with a hammer.

The placement of your shade determines the type of brackets you'll need. One type serves an inside-mounted shade; another type is for an outside mount. Both work with either a conventional-roll or a reverse-roll shade.

A wood slat such as screen door molding, cut 1/2 inch shorter than the finished width of the shade, serves as a bottom support and weight.

METAL AND CARDBOARD ROLLERS
SHIRRING TAPE
SHADE CORD
SLATS
SHADE RINGS
SCREW EYES
CLEATS
SHADE PULLS
MOUNTING BOARDS
BRACKETS
FUSIBLE BACKING

Typical hardware for shades includes metal rollers that must be bought to size and sturdy cardboard and wood rollers that can be cut to the necessary length.

flat roman shade

Though nearly flat when unfurled, this basic Roman shade draws up into graceful, horizontal folds. The accordion effect is accomplished by pulling cords that run through rings attached to the back of the shade.

Because it hugs the window, a flat Roman shade insulates well. For even more protection, you can interline your shade as long as the interlining won't require seaming (the seams would show). Cut the interlining to the finished width and length, with the allowance at the top for going over the board. Slip the interlining under the pressed side and lower hems, and treat the panel as one.

PLANNING. Decide on an inside or outside mount and note the hardware you'll need (see page 70). Typical vertical spacing between rings is 6 to 8 inches—you determine the exact vertical spacing as you make the shade. Typical horizontal spacing of rings is from 9 to 14 inches, depending on the width of the shade and where any seams fall. Typical skirt length is 6 inches.

If you need to join fabric widths, center a full width and add partial widths to the sides (to match pattern repeats when seaming widths, see page 23). Also, when determining where to seam your fabric, keep in mind that you should have a row of rings at each seam; you may need to adjust the horizontal spacing slightly.

CHOOSING FABRIC. Traditionally, Roman shades are lined and made in firmly woven fabrics to enable the horizontal folds to be crisp and hold their shape. But now, loosely woven fabrics, even sheers, are used to create soft-folded looks.

CALCULATING YARDAGE. Measure your window and fill in the window treatment work sheet (see pages 16–18). A Roman shade has no fullness or returns. For each seam, add a 1-inch allowance to your finished-width figure.

Finished length for an inside-mounted shade equals the length of the opening; for an outside mount, finished length is the length of the opening, plus the distance above and/or below, plus the shade's skirt.

For a patterned fabric with a repeat, plan to place a full repeat at the bottom of the skirt.

Use the following allowances in your calculations (assuming a 6-inch skirt length):

	FABRIC	LINING
TOP	3"	3"
SIDE HEMS	3" TOTAL	1" TOTAL
SKIRT HEM	6"	5½"
LOWER HEM (IF NO SKIRT)	1½"	1"

FLAT ROMAN SHADE STEP-BY-STEP

1 Choose and prepare face fabric and lining, and join the fabric widths (see pages 21–23). Press seams open.

2 With face fabric wrong side up, fold over each side edge 1½ inches, wrong side in; press. On lining, press under 1 inch on each side edge. Fold up lower skirt hem on face fabric 6 inches (if no skirt, fold up 1½ inches); press. Repeat for lining, folding up 5½ inches (1 inch if no skirt).

3 Lay face fabric, wrong side up, on work surface. Unfold skirt and make a small horizontal tuck in each side hem near lower hem fold, causing side hems to widen and angle in about ½ inch.

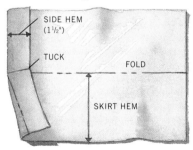

4 Fold hem up again. Place lining, right side up, on face fabric so top edges are aligned and lining is $^1\!/_2$ inch from side and lower edges. Raw edges of face fabric and lining hems should be aligned.

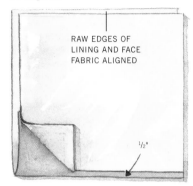

RAW EDGES OF LINING AND FACE FABRIC ALIGNED

$^1\!/_2$"

5 Carefully fold back lining to expose raw edges of both hems. Without shifting layers, pin together hems only; stitch $1^1\!/_2$ inches from raw edges.

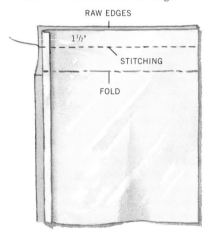

RAW EDGES

$1^1\!/_2$"

STITCHING

FOLD

6 Bring lining back over face fabric; pin layers together along sides and across top of skirt. Stitch through all layers $^1\!/_4$ inch below enclosed raw edges of face fabric and lining skirts (you can usually see raw edges through lining), creating a $1^1\!/_4$-inch hidden rod pocket (match top thread to lining and bobbin thread to face fabric).

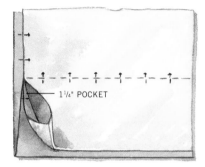

$1^1\!/_4$" POCKET

7 With layers still pinned together and lining side up, stitch down right side, beginning at top right edge and making a $^3\!/_4$-inch seam. Stop stitching at rod-pocket stitching. Repeat on other side, beginning at rod-pocket stitching.

8 On right side of shade, measure finished length from bottom of hem and mark with pins every 4 inches across width. Measure and trim top allowance to $1^1\!/_4$ inches. Fold down top, lining side in, along pin-marked finished-length line and press. Remove pins.

9 To join lining and face fabric, serge or zigzag top edge.

10 To determine positions for rings, measure width from side hem to side hem and divide by desired spacing (9 to 14 inches); round off to nearest whole number to get number of spaces. Divide width by number of spaces to arrive at exact space size. If fabric is seamed, adjust so a row of rings falls on each seam.

With lining side up, use space size to mark vertical lines, starting at rod-pocket stitching and extending to top. Pin lining to face fabric along marked lines, placing pins perpendicular to lines.

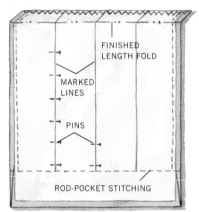

FINISHED LENGTH FOLD

MARKED LINES

PINS

ROD-POCKET STITCHING

11 Sew a straight seam over each marked line.

12 To find vertical space between rings, divide distance from top of pocket to top fold by desired vertical spacing (6 to 8 inches). Round off to nearest whole number to get number of spaces. Divide same distance by number of spaces to arrive at exact space size.

Mark ring positions with pins, aligning pins horizontally.

13 Using doubled polyester thread to match lining, sew bottom rings at rod-pocket stitching line and other rings at markings with buttonhole stitch. Sew through the lining only.

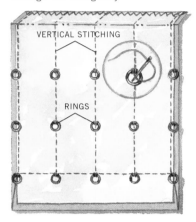

14 Insert rod in pocket and slipstitch pocket closed, continuing along edge of lining on each side. Also slipstitch angled face fabric to each side.

15 To cover mounting board, cut a piece of fabric 1 inch wider than the distance around board and 5 inches longer on each end. Fold and staple fabric to board.

Position shade right side up over board so finished-length fold aligns with top front edge of board (for an inside or outside mount, face of board is up; for a flat mount on a door, face is against door). Staple top allowance to board.

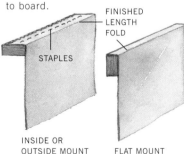

16 Turn shade and board wrong side up. Insert screw eyes in board $^{3}/_{4}$ inch from front edge ($^{3}/_{8}$ inch on a flat-mounted shade) and above each row of rings.

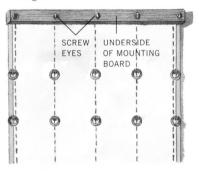

17 For each row of rings, cut a separate length of cord long enough to go through a row of rings, across top of shade to left, and halfway down side (instructions are for a shade with cords on right; to place cords on left, run cords to right).

18 With shade still wrong side up, tie one end of cord to bottom left ring and thread cord up through all rings in row; pass cord from right to left through screw eye at top and let remainder of cord hang down left side. Repeat for all rows of rings.

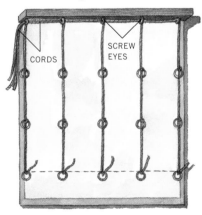

19 Before hanging, lay shade flat, pull cords to draw shade up to board, and secure cords. Straighten horizontal folds and lightly crease with your hands. When folds are arranged, tie with fabric strips every 6 to 8 inches; keep tied for three or four days.

20 With shade unfurled, adjust tension of cords so shade draws up in even horizontal folds when cords are pulled. Lower shade and knot cords together just below right-hand screw eye.

Divide cords; braid to within 2 inches of end of shortest cord. Put cords through shade pull, knot, and trim ends. Slide pull over knot. To secure cords, mount a cleat on the window frame.

21 *For an inside mount,* screw board directly into window frame (narrow edge faces out).

For an outside mount, measure from ceiling to position of angle iron ($^{3}/_{4}$ inch lower than top of board) on one side; also measure proper distance to side of opening. Install angle iron. Lay one end of board over angle iron. Place a carpenter's level on top of board at other end; adjust board until level. Mark position of other angle iron; install.

For a flat mount on a door, lift up shade and screw the board into the door, using a carpenter's level to check the alignment.

swagged roman shade

A swagged Roman shade is a loose variation of a traditional Roman shade. Often made in soft or semisheer fabrics, many times unlined, the shade is drawn up in fewer places, thus forming a center swag and side tails.

For a standard casement window, sew a row of vertical rings about 6 inches in from each side to make a single swag and two tails.

When using this treatment continuously over a double window or multiple windows, plan the ring settings to correspond with the window framing or mullions. Adjust the placement of the rings if necesary so the swags are no wider than 36 inches.

stitched roman shade

Stitching along the edge of folds on both the front and back of the shade creates neat horizontal tucks in this tailored Roman shade. The stitching acts as a memory for the folds.

PLANNING. See "Flat Roman shade," page 71, for general planning guidelines. Because of the stack, it's better to mount this shade outside the window frame.

CHOOSING FABRIC. Fabrics that form a crisp fold are best.

CALCULATING YARDAGE. Calculate yardage as you would for a flat Roman shade, adding in fabric for the tucks.

1 Determine finished length; subtract skirt length.

2 Divide result by desired space size (from 6 to 8 inches); round off to nearest whole number to get number of spaces. Divide same distance by number of spaces to arrive at exact space size.

3 Multiply number of spaces by 2 inches (1 inch for each front and back tuck) and add to finished length. Add 1 inch for tuck take-up.

STITCHED ROMAN SHADE STEP-BY-STEP

1 Follow steps 1–7, "Flat Roman shade," pages 71–72, to make hems and rod pocket.

2 On back of shade, measure ½ inch from rod-pocket stitching. Pin across width every 4 inches through both layers. From pin-marked line, measure space size plus 2 inches and pin across width. Repeat up shade one less time than number of spaces.

Remaining distance should equal space size plus 1½ inches.

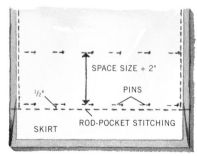

3 Fold on bottom row of pins, face fabric in. Remove pins and press fold. Repin, placing the pins perpendicular to the fold.

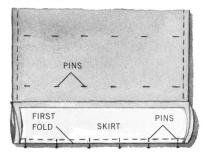

4 Make next fold on next row of pins. Repeat for all rows up back of shade.

5 Stitch each fold $1/2$ inch from folded edge, using thread to match lining; on bottom fold, stitch just to left of rod-pocket stitching.

6 Starting at bottom, bring bottom two tucks together. Crease center fold on front, and pin perpendicular to fold. Repeat for remaining front tucks. Stitch as for back tucks, using thread to match face fabric.

7 Follow steps 8–9, "Flat Roman shade," page 72, to measure finished length and to finish top edge.

8 Follow first part of step 10, "Flat Roman shade," page 72 to determine spacing for rings across the width. Mark positions for rings on back tucks.

9 Using doubled polyester thread to match lining, sew rings through tucks on back with buttonhole stitch.

10 Follow steps 14–21, "Flat Roman shade," page 73, to finish shade.

doweled roman shade

A doweled Roman shade is constructed in the same way as a stitched Roman shade except that a rod is inserted in the front tucks only. Cut $3/8$-inch-diameter wood dowel rods, flat screen door molding, or small PVC pipe $1/2$ inch shorter than the finished width of the blind. To determine the tuck size, wrap scraps of fabric and lining around the diameter of the rod and measure the distance between the meeting points, leaving some ease for the rod to move into the pocket. Adjust your yardage calculations accordingly.

After you have constructed the shade, insert the rods into the front only tucks and slipstitch the ends.

ADDING A VALANCE

A valance is a decorative trim, either straight or shaped, constructed as a separate piece and mounted at the top of a Roman shade. A valance should be about one-fifth of the total height of the shade and the same width.

1 To the finished size of the valance, add $1^{1}/_{2}$ inches for the top allowance, $1^{1}/_{2}$ inches for the lower hem, and 3 inches total for side hems.

2 Construct the side hems first, then the lower hem; serge the top edge. (The valance may be lined, if desired.)

3 Install the shade onto the header board, and staple the top allowance of the valance over it.

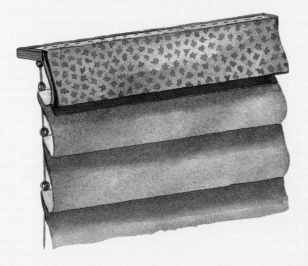

soft-fold roman shade

Loops of fabric flow down the face of this shade, even when it's lowered. Extra fabric between the rings means the folds stay softly rounded.

This version takes more time to make and requires more fabric than a flat Roman shade, but the extra fabric makes a great insulator whether the shade is mounted inside or outside the window frame.

The distinctive horizontal lines created by the folds add a custom note to these shades.

PLANNING. Follow the planning guidelines for "Flat Roman shade," page 71, with these additional typical dimensions: Vertical spacing between rings is 5 inches, the distance between folds (seen from the front) is 5 inches, each loop of fabric that becomes a soft fold takes 9 inches, and skirt length is equal to the distance between rings, plus 2 inches (7 inches in example below).

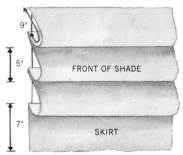

9"

5"

7"

FRONT OF SHADE

SKIRT

To determine the exact vertical space between rings, subtract the skirt length from the finished length and divide by the desired spacing between rings; round off to the nearest whole number for the number of spaces. Divide the finished length less the skirt length by the number of spaces for the exact space size. Each loop will be 4 inches more.

You'll space rings 9 to 14 inches apart horizontally, depending on the width of the shade and where any seams fall.

CHOOSING FABRIC. Many fabrics suitable for flat Roman shades will also work for this shade. The fabric must be supple enough to form the loops but not so soft that the loops flatten.

CALCULATING YARDAGE. Measure your window and fill in the window treatment work sheet (see pages 16–18). A soft-fold Roman shade has no fullness or returns. For each seam, add a 1-inch allowance to your finished-width figure.

To determine the cut length of the face fabric, one easy method is simply to double the finished length of the shade. This allows for plenty of fabric to go over the board and create the soft folds and skirt. Calculate lining fabric separately, adding the top allowance and skirt to the finished length. The lining is not part of the folding system and remains flat as in a flat Roman shade.

Use the following allowances in your calculations (assuming a 7-inch skirt length):

	FABRIC	LINING
TOP	3"	3"
SIDE HEMS	6" TOTAL	3" TOTAL
SKIRT HEM	7"	6½"

SOFT-FOLD ROMAN SHADE STEP-BY-STEP

1 Choose and prepare face fabric and lining, and join the fabric widths (see pages 21–23). Press the seams open.

2 Fold over each side edge of face fabric 3 inches, wrong side in; press. Turn in raw edge to meet pressed fold and press again. Repeat on lining, folding over each side edge 2 inches.

3 Fold up lower skirt hem on face fabric 7 inches, wrong side in; press. Repeat on the lining, folding up 6½ inches.

4 Follow steps 3–6, "Flat Roman shade," pages 71–72, to make tucks and stitch rod pocket.

5 Lay shade, right side up, on work surface. From stitching at top of rod pocket, measure up 2 inches on face fabric and mark with pins across width, pinning through face fabric *only*.

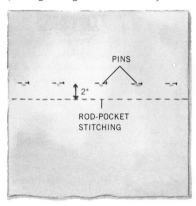

Fold on the pin-marked line and pull down the "loop" of fabric to create the first fold.

6 From pin-marked line, measure up distance to be seen between folds plus 2 inches (7 inches in example). Pin across width through face fabric *and* lining; place masking tape across width so lower edge of tape is on pin-marked line.

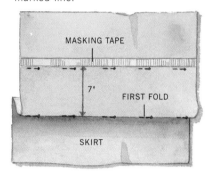

7 Measure up 2 more inches from pin-marked line on face fabric, and pin across width through face fabric *only*.

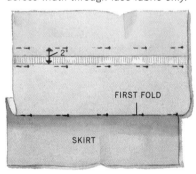

Fold on upper pin-marked line and pull down loop of fabric for second fold.

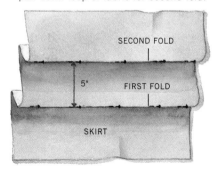

8 Repeat steps 6 and 7, ending with step 7, to form the required number of folds.

9 At second loop from bottom, lift and stitch through face fabric and lining along lower edge of tape, removing pins as you go. Repeat up face of shade. Remove tape.

10 Follow steps 8–9, "Flat Roman shade," page 72, to measure finished length and finish top edge.

11 Follow first part of step 10, "Flat Roman shade," page 72, to mark positions for rings with pins, making sure rings align vertically (bottom rings go on rod-pocket stitching, remaining rings on horizontal rows of stitching),

12 Using doubled polyester thread to match lining, sew rings to lining only with a buttonhole stitch.

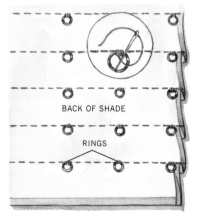

13 Follow steps 14–18 and 20–21, "Flat Roman shade," page 73, to finish the shade.

balloon shade

True to its name, a balloon shade is airy and rounded, with deep inverted pleats that fall into poufs at the bottom. You draw the shade up using cords threaded through rings. On some balloon shades, the bottom pouf remains when the shade is completely lowered, an effect that is achieved by adding to the length and tying the lower rings together.

PLANNING. This project is for an outside-mounted balloon shade. Note the hardware and notions you'll need (see page 70).

On a balloon shade, each fabric width will make a half-pleat, a space, a full pleat, a space, and another half-pleat (size depends on board size and usable fabric widths).

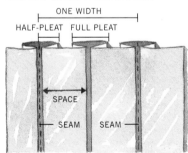

For unpatterned fabric or fabric with an allover pattern, start with a trial space size of 10 inches. If your fabric has large motifs, carefully analyze the design and choose space and pleat sizes that will place the desired part of the pattern in each of the spaces.

You'll add returns to cover the ends of the board once you've seamed the widths. A half-pleat extends to each end of the face board; the return and side hem are beyond.

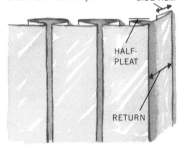

Vertical spacing of rings can range from 6 to 10 inches, depending on how deep you want the folds.

CHOOSING FABRIC. Select a fabric that's firm enough to hold pleats and soft enough to form poufs.

CALCULATING YARDAGE. Follow these steps to arrive at pleat and space sizes and yards needed. In the following example, the board is $1\frac{1}{2}$ inches wide by 48 inches long and the fabric is 54 inches wide.

1 Measure your window and fill in the window treatment work sheet (pages 16–18) to arrive at board size. Return size is equal to depth of board.

2 Divide board size by 10 inches (trial space size); round off to nearest whole number for number of spaces (48 ÷ 10 = 4.8, rounds to 5). Divide board size by number of spaces for exact space size (48 ÷ 5 = 9.6 or $9\frac{5}{8}$ inches).

3 Subtract exact space size from half the usable fabric width (26 inches for fabric with 52 inches usable fabric) for pleat loop size ($26 - 9\frac{5}{8} = 16\frac{3}{8}$ inches). When flattened, each full pleat will be half the loop size (about $8\frac{1}{8}$ inches).

4 To determine number of fabric widths needed, divide number of spaces (from step 2) by 2. If result is a whole number, add a width; if result contains a half-width, round up to next whole number. Continue to fill in second row of work sheet.

Also use the following allowances in your calculations:

	FABRIC	LINING
TOP	3"	3"
LOWER HEM with pouf	21"	18"
without pouf	3"	NONE

BALLOON SHADE STEP-BY-STEP

1 Choose and prepare face fabric and lining (see pages 21–23).

2 *If you have an odd number of spaces,* join fabric widths as described on page 23; press seams open. Lay face fabric right side up; measure, mark, and trim a quarter-width from the width at far right. Pin and stitch this piece to the width at far left.

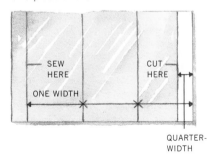

Press seam open. From this seam, measure, mark, and trim fabric a distance equal to return plus $1\frac{1}{2}$ inches. From right seam, measure a distance equal to a half-width; from this point, measure, mark, and cut fabric a distance equal to return plus $1\frac{1}{2}$ inches. Repeat on the lining so seams will align with those on the face fabric; trim 1 inch on each side.

If you have an even number of spaces, join all widths except one. Split this width and sew half to one side and half to other side; press seams open. From each end seam, measure and mark toward edge a distance equal to return plus $1\frac{1}{2}$ inches; cut fabric. Repeat on lining so seams will align with those on face fabric; trim 1 inch on each side.

3 Fold over each side edge of face fabric $1\frac{1}{2}$ inches, wrong side in; press. Repeat on lining, folding over each side edge 1 inch.

4 Lay face fabric wrong side up. Place lining, right side up, on face fabric $\frac{1}{2}$ inch in from side edges; lower edge of lining should be 3 inches above lower edge of face fabric. Pin together at side edges and stitch, making a $\frac{3}{4}$-inch seam and continuing stitching to lower edge of face fabric (match top thread to lining and bobbin to face fabric).

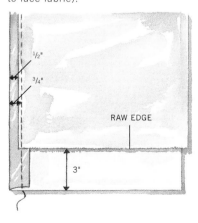

5 With lining still right side up, measure and mark vertical lines for rows of stitching and rings at midpoint of each full width. For a shade with an odd number of spaces, also measure and mark a line where return begins on unseamed side edge. Pin all seams and marked lines. Beginning at raw edge of lining at lower hem, stitch over marked lines and seams.

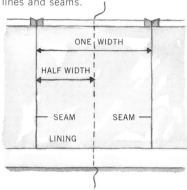

6 Turn shade right side up and, on right edge, measure from line of return stitching toward center a distance equal to a half-pleat loop; pin vertically down length of shade.

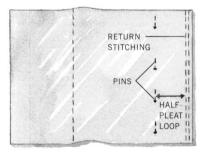

To form half-pleat, bring pin-marked line to return stitching. Pin layers together close to front and back folds.

Repeat on other edge.

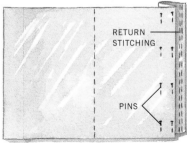

7 Measure and mark same distance on either side of each row of vertical stitching. To form a full pleat, bring each pin-marked line to row of stitching; pin in place vertically near front folds so pleats "kiss." Space size must be as determined earlier; adjust pleats if necessary.

Pin through all layers where pleats form folds on back.

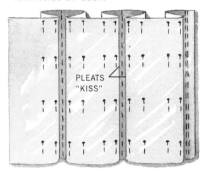

8 Turn shade lining side up. To hold pleats in place, edgestitch all folds from raw edge of lining to lower edge of face fabric, backstitching at beginning and end.

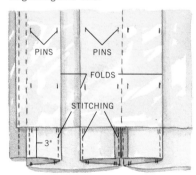

9 At bottom edge, turn up face fabric 3 inches; press. Turn raw edge in to meet pressed fold and press again. Stitch lower hem close to second fold to form rod pocket.

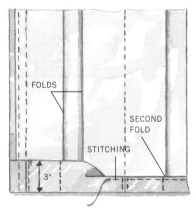

10 Turn shade right side up. On one edge, fold back return along return stitching. Then, fold edge of shade forward to meet return stitching, forming a ³/₄-inch pleat. On the wrong side, hand-stitch pleat to lower edge of pocket.

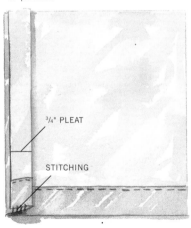

11 On right side of shade, measure finished length from bottom of hem and mark with pins every 4 inches across width. Measure and trim top allowances ¹/₄ inch narrower than board. Fold down top allowance, lining side in, along pin-marked finished-length line; press. Remove the pins. Press the pleats in place above the finished-length line.

To join face fabric and lining, serge or zigzag top edge.

12 With pins, mark each ring position, aligning rings horizontally (rings will be sewn to side hem stitching and vertical stitching, but not return stitching). Place bottom rings at top of rod pocket and other rings 6 to 10 inches apart.

13 Follow step 13, "Flat Roman shade," page 73, to sew on rings, being careful not to catch side edges of pleats.

14 Cover one end of the rod with masking tape and insert in pocket; slipstitch closed. Form a ³/₄-inch pleat, same as on other end; hand-stitch the pleat to lower edge of pocket.

15 Follow steps 15–18 and 20–21, "Flat Roman shade," page 73, with these changes or additions: In step 15, fold and staple return portion of top allowance to each board end; in step 18, tie together lower four rings in each row to create pouf; in step 20, disregard reference to folds.

london shade

A London shade is a cousin to the swagged Roman shade in looks, but it is made like a balloon shade, with just two inverted pleats widely spaced and the side rigging omitted. The soft scallop and tails are formed when the two bottom rows of rigging rings are tied together. As the shade is raised, the scalloping and draping increase, creating an even softer look.

cloud shade

Soft shirring across the top differentiates the cloud shade from the balloon shade. The tape used to achieve this look comes in a variety of patterns, from simple gathers to pencil pleats and smocking. Rings are attached to the back of the shade; when the shade is drawn up, gentle scallops form.

PLANNING. This project is for an outside-mounted cloud shade. Note the hardware and notions you'll need (see page 70). Buy shirring tape equal in length to total shade width. Two-cord tape, the narrowest, creates about an inch of shirring; four-cord tape creates about 4 inches.

For the heading (the ruffle above the shirring), choose a size according to the width of the tape. With two-cord tape, a 2- to 3-inch heading is appropriate. With three- or four-cord tape, the heading is usually $1/2$ inch.

Vertical spacing of the rings can range from 6 to 10 inches, depending on the depth of the folds.

To create a base for the rings on an unlined sheer shade, take $1/4$-inch vertical tucks midway between seams joining widths. Press the tucks to one side and stitch them down. Sew the rings to the tucks, keeping vertical spacing equal.

CHOOSING FABRIC. A cloud shade made from a crisp fabric will hold its shape and provide good light control and privacy. One made from batiste, gauze, or lace will hang in soft folds and filter light.

CALCULATING YARDAGE. The following project assumes a $1^{1}/_2$-inch-wide board.

1 Measure your window and fill in window treatment work sheet (see pages 16–18) to arrive at board size. Add 3 inches for two $1^{1}/_2$-inch returns. (If, for example, your board is 60 inches long, adjusted board size would be 63 inches.)

2 Divide adjusted board size by 10 inches (trial space size); round off to nearest whole number for number of spaces (63 ÷ 10 = 6.3, rounds to 6).

3 To determine number of widths, divide number of spaces by 2 (each width of fabric will make two spaces, or scallops); if result contains a half-width, round up to next whole number.

Continue to fill in second row of work sheet, using number of widths just determined. Use following allowances in your calculations:

	FABRIC	LINING
TOP	HEADING SIZE + $1/2$"	NONE
LOWER HEMS	21"	18"

CLOUD SHADE STEP-BY-STEP

1 Choose and prepare face fabric and lining; and join the fabric widths (see pages 21–23) so the seams on face fabric and lining will align. Press seams open.

2 For an odd number of spaces, measure and cut a half-width from right or left width on face fabric. Trim lining 1 inch narrower than face fabric on each side.

3 Follow steps 3–4, "Balloon shade," page 79, to join lining and face fabric and to make side hems.

4 With lining right side up, measure and mark vertical lines for rows of stitching at midpoint of each full width. Pin marked lines and seams. Beginning at raw edge of lining at lower hem, stitch over marked lines and seams.

5 At bottom edge, turn up face fabric 3 inches; press. Turn raw edge in to meet pressed fold and press again. Stitch lower hem close to second fold to form rod pocket.

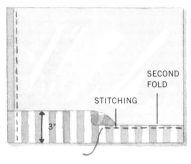

6 Follow step 12, "Balloon shade," page 80, to mark ring positions (disregard reference to return stitching).

7 On right side of shade, measure finished length from bottom of hem and mark with pins every 4 inches across width. Measure proper top allowance beyond finished-length line; trim. Remove stitching at top of each side hem to finished-length line. Trim lining so upper edge meets pin-marked line.

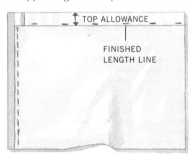

8 Fold down top allowance, wrong side in, on finished-length line; press. Remove pins. Position shirring tape, right side up, on back of shade, turning under ends and placing top edge ³⁄₄ inch above raw edge.

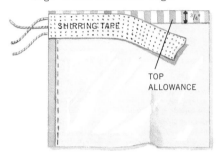

Pin, stitch, and gather tape following manufacturer's instructions (shirred heading should equal adjusted board size).

9 Follow step 13, "Flat Roman shade," page 73, to sew on rings.

10 Follow first part of step 15, "Flat Roman shade," page 73, to cover mounting board.

11 Staple shade to face and ends of mounting board, placing staples vertically 2 inches apart and concealing them between gathers. Insert rod in pocket and slipstitch closed.

12 Follow steps 16–18, "Flat Roman shade," page 73. In step 18, tie together lower four rings in each row to create pouf.

13 Follow steps 20–21, "Flat Roman shade," page 73, to finish shade (disregard reference to folds in step 20).

ruffled cloud shade

A ruffled bottom adds a frilly detail to a cloud shade. You'll need extra fabric for the ruffle. Fold and press side hems on face fabric and lining. Make a folded ruffle for the lower edge (see pages 42–43). Pin to right side of face fabric. Baste, making a ¹⁄₂-inch seam.

Center lining over face fabric and ruffle and sew a ¹⁄₂-inch seam.

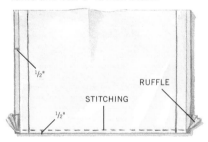

Turn face fabric and lining right sides out and lightly press. With lining side up, pin side and lower edges together. Starting at upper right and making a ³⁄₄-inch seam, stitch down side edge, across bottom, and up other side, pivoting at corners. Follow steps 7–13, "Cloud shade," to finish.

roller shade

Of all the shade styles, the roller shade requires the least amount of fabric and sewing—there are no seams, side hems, folds, or gathers. And, because the shade is flat, the fabric's pattern shows clearly. A top treatment, such as a valance or narrow cornice, finishes the shade nicely and hides the roller.

Two cautions: The width of the roller shade can't exceed the usable width of your fabric—splitting or seaming is glaringly obvious and interferes with the smooth operation of the shade. Also, roller shades are not recommended for windows more than 5 feet high.

PLANNING AND INSTALLATION.
Choose the type of roll and mounting before you purchase hardware or fabric. Because you won't know the thickness of the shade until it's finished, make the shade before installing the brackets. When you install them, be sure to position them so the roller will be perfectly level.

For a conventional-roll shade, the blade end of the roller should be on your left as you face the window. Mount the slotted bracket on the left side and the other bracket on the right. *For a reverse-roll shade,* reverse the brackets.

CHOOSING FABRIC AND BACKING.
Look for a firmly woven all-cotton or other natural-fiber fabric that won't fray easily. Avoid fabrics with heavy finishes, which may prevent the backing from adhering to the fabric.

If selecting a blend that contains synthetic fibers, test samples of fabric and backing to make sure the fabric bonds well before purchasing the entire amount of fabric.

Fusible shade backing, a heat-sensitive material made especially for shades, stiffens the fabric and, if it's a blackout backing, blocks light. Backings come in varying widths; look for them in fabric stores.

CALCULATING YARDAGE. The finished width of your shade is equal to the desired length of the roller. The piece of fabric must be 3 inches wider than the finished shade width and 12 inches longer than the finished length (for wrapping around the roller). If the fabric has repeats, buy enough to place a full repeat just above the slat and to center a repeat horizontally. Purchase a piece of fusible backing the same size as the fabric.

ROLLER SHADE STEP-BY-STEP

1 Choose and prepare face fabric (see pages 21–22).

2 Square off one end of face fabric. Measure total length of shade; square and cut other end.

3 Fuse the shade fabric and backing, following the manufacturer's instructions and working from center to outside and from top to bottom.

4 Measure and mark side edges to finished width, keeping lines straight and corners square. Cut along lines with a rotary cutter or sharp scissors, making long, clean strokes and keeping fabric perfectly flat.

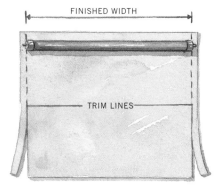

FINISHED WIDTH

TRIM LINES

5 Turn up lower edge 1 1/2 inches, backing side in; finger-press fold. Stitch 1 1/4 inches from edge, using longest straight-stitch setting. Insert a wood slat in pocket.

6 Align top edge of shade with guideline on roller (if roller has no guideline, hold roller firmly on a table and, with marker lying flat on table, draw a line along roller.)

7 Attach shade to roller with masking tape, aligning edge with guideline; be sure orientation is correct for conventional or reverse roll. To check that shade is straight, roll by hand and insert in brackets. If shade is crooked, unroll and adjust. If roller is wood, staple shade to roller using 1/4-inch staples; pound in staples with a hammer if necessary.

8 To prevent fraying, put a small amount of liquid fray preventer on your finger and draw it along the edge; let dry completely before raising shade.

valances

ABOVE: A band of subtle plaid trims
a long gathered arched valance of
shimmering gold silk. The longer the
valance, the more it needs side panels
to balance the treatment.

OPPOSITE: This scalloped valance is
attached to a wood rod with rings.
Lined to the edge and with no visible
stitching lines, the valance has a
streamlined look. Playful fringe
outlines the graceful, undulating edge.

LEFT: The cheerful fruit print is not lost in the folds of a balloon valance mounted on an over-the-sink kitchen window. A balloon valance is a non-functioning balloon shade.

BELOW: The contrasting heading and ruffle on this cloud valance add a striking counterpoint to the large-scale "balloon" print. A cloud valance works well over stationary side panels.

A billowy cloud valance topped with a ruffle is just the right touch to soften the angular lines of a built-in window seat and surrounding bookcases. The lightweight fabric doesn't block the view and welcomes in the sunlight.

ABOVE: The end pleats are buttoned
back to expose contrasting fabric on
this crisp plaid kick-pleated valance
that tops corner windows. The precise
look is achieved by careful measuring
and planning to ensure that the pleats
align perfectly with the plaid's grid.

RIGHT: A large-scale fruit and floral
print is an unexpected but successful
pattern to use on a pleated valance.
A contrasting striped fabric, used for
the bottom edging and a knotted cord
trim on the top, provides a nice accent.

ABOVE: This variation on a stagecoach valance features a large scallop made by drawing up the fabric in two places. Tabs made of fabric-covered cords knotted together add interest. Note how the scallop shape of the valance echoes the top curve of the window.

RIGHT: A rolled stagecoach valance mounted higher than the window frame makes this window opening appear larger than it actually is. The all-natural look features a textured linen fabric with checkered tabs.

how to make valances

Whether used alone or with other treatments, fabric valances soften and frame windows. Some valances, such as rod-pocket and balloon valances, can be thought of simply as shortened curtains or shades; other valances are unique. Shaped valances add a graceful inner curve to the window while straight valances finish off the top edge. All valances used over another treatment help conceal the hardware.

Though styles may be different, most valances call for an attached lining at the lower hem. Sewing the lining in with the face fabric at the lower edge ensures a neat, professional look.

fabric needs

Often you'll use the same fabric for the valance as for the undertreatment. Where there's no undertreatment, or if the valance is made from a contrasting fabric, follow the fabric guidelines for the longer version. Also take a look at the individual project for specific recommendations.

length guidelines

Most valances begin 8 inches above the window opening, though this can vary depending on what's underneath. Finished length for straight valances is from 12 to 18 inches; shaped valances can be considerably longer on the sides, sometimes reaching to the sill.

Long valances can reduce light, interfere with the view, and visually shorten windows. If you like the look of a deep valance, consider starting it farther above the window opening.

hardware

Rod-pocket and related shaped valances hang from curtain rods (see at left and page 36); install the rod as described on page 37. The rod can be mounted on the inside or outside of the window frame, depending on the look you want. Other valances, such as pleated and balloon styles, are board-mounted. A valance used alone requires a board at least 1¹/₂ inches deep; one used over other treatments requires a board deep enough to clear whatever is underneath and to cover up the hardware used for the undertreatment.

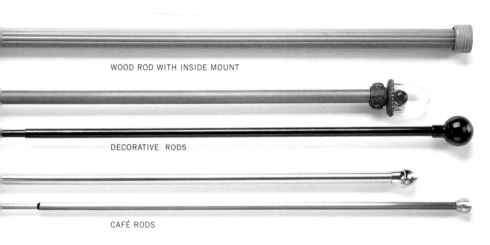

WOOD ROD WITH INSIDE MOUNT

DECORATIVE RODS

CAFÉ RODS

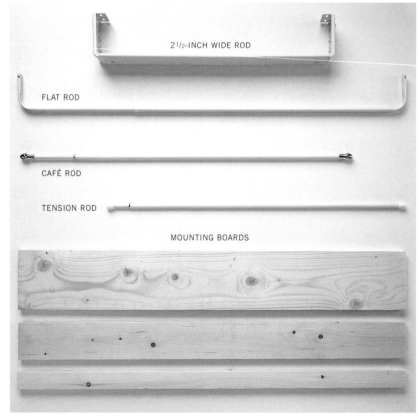

2¹/₂-INCH WIDE ROD

FLAT ROD

CAFÉ ROD

TENSION ROD

MOUNTING BOARDS

Hardware for valances includes decorative curtain and drapery rods, basic curtain rods, and mounting boards, each appropriate for different styles of valances.

rod-pocket valance

This basic valance style looks just like a short rod-pocket curtain, but the order of fabrication is different, and the lining hem is attached.

CALCULATING YARDAGE. Measure your window and fill in the window treatment work sheet (see pages 16–18). For most fabrics, a fullness of 3 times the finished width is best. For length guidelines, see page 90.

Use the following allowances in your calculations. Refer to the top chart on page 46 for pocket size.

	FABRIC	**LINING**
LOWER HEMS	3"	1½"
SIDE HEMS	5" TOTAL	NONE
TOP	2 × POCKET + 2 × HEADING (IF USED)	NONE

ROD-POCKET VALANCE STEP-BY-STEP

1 Choose and prepare face fabric and lining, joining fabric widths as described (see pages 21–23). Press seams open.

2 With right sides together, pin and stitch face fabric and lining at lower edge, centering the lining on the face fabric and making a 1½-inch seam. Press seam allowances toward face fabric. Press lower hem so 1½ inches of face fabric shows on back.

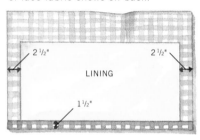

3 On right side of face fabric, measure from lower edge a distance equal to finished length and mark with pins every 4 inches across valance. Measure and mark proper top allowance (2 times pocket plus 2 times heading, if desired) above pin-marked finished-length line. Trim ravel allowance. Trim lining so upper edge meets pin-marked finished-length line.

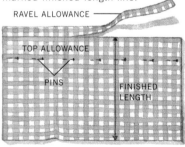

4 For side hems, turn face fabric 2½ inches to the wrong side and press. Turn raw edge in to meet pressed fold and press again. Fold corners diagonally to form miter. Blindhem by machine or hand-slipstitch hem to lining only.

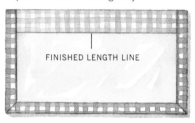

5 Fold top edge of fabric, wrong side in, along finished-length line; press. Remove pins. Turn raw edge in to meet the pressed fold and press again. Stitch close to the second fold. For heading, if used, stitch again from the top fold a distance equal to the heading depth; press.

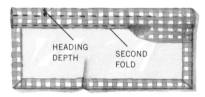

6 Slip rod through pocket between back two layers of fabric, gathering fabric evenly.

pouf valance

Sometimes called a mock balloon, a pouf valance has a rod pocket at the top and is double-layered to allow the fabric to spread apart into crisp peaks and poufs.

CALCULATING YARDAGE. Measure your window and fill in the window treatment work sheet (see pages 16–18). For most fabrics, a fullness of 3 times the finished width is best.

To determine finished length, make a sketch of your window. Finished length is equal to the distance covered above the window opening, plus the amount that extends into the opening times 2.

Typically, a valance used alone or over an inside-mounted treatment starts 8 inches above the opening, extends 4 inches into the opening and doubles back on itself completely. (Finished length in example is 24 inches.)

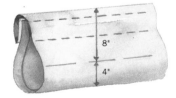

A valance over draperies might start 15 inches above the opening (near or at the ceiling) and extend 3 inches into the opening.

Use the following allowances in your calculations. Refer to the top chart on page 46 for pocket size.

	FABRIC	LINING
LOWER HEMS	POCKET + HEADING	POCKET + HEADING
SIDE HEMS	5" TOTAL	NONE
TOP	3 × POCKET + 3 × HEADING (IF USED)	3 × POCKET + 3 × HEADING (IF USED)

POUF VALANCE STEP-BY-STEP

1 Choose and prepare face fabric and lining, and join the fabric widths (see pages 21–23). Press seams open. On right side of face fabric, measure from lower edge a distance equal to finished length. Mark with pins every 4 inches across valance.

2 Center lining on face fabric, wrong sides together, aligning top and bottom raw edges. For side hems, turn face fabric 2½ inches to the wrong side and press. Turn raw edge in to meet pressed fold and press again. Blindhem by machine or hand-slipstitch hem to lining only.

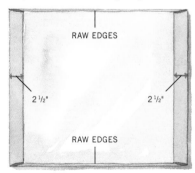

RAW EDGES

2½"   2½"

RAW EDGES

3 Measure and mark across top allowance (3 times pocket plus 3 times heading, if used) above pin-marked finished-length line. Trim ravel allowance.

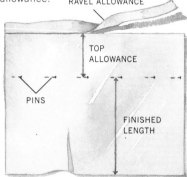

RAVEL ALLOWANCE

TOP ALLOWANCE

PINS

FINISHED LENGTH

4 Fold top allowance to wrong side along pin-marked finished-length line; press. Fold raw edge in to meet pressed fold and press again. Remove pins. Fold entire piece, lining side in, tucking in bottom raw edge until it meets first fold. Stitch close to second fold. For heading, if used, stitch again from top fold a distance equal to heading depth; press.

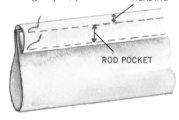

HEADING

ROD POCKET

5 Slip rod through pocket between back two layers of fabric, gathering fabric evenly. Pull layers apart to create pouf. Add crumpled tissue paper, if you like, to help keep the pouf shape.

arched valance

This gathered valance forms a graceful curve along its lower edge. The arch should be gentle; a sharply arched valance, when gathered, won't curve evenly along its lower edge.

CALCULATING YARDAGE. Measure your window and fill in the window treatment work sheet (see pages 16–18). For most fabrics, a fullness of 3 times the finished width is best. Finished length is the longest point at the sides.

For best appearance, the difference between the long and short points of the arch should be no more than 8 inches and no less than 3 inches. A typical finished side length is 18 inches, with a finished center length of 10 inches.

Use the following allowances in your calculations. Refer to the top chart on page 46 for pocket size. If you plan to add a ruffle, piping, or facing, buy extra fabric.

	FABRIC	LINING
LOWER HEMS	½"	½"
SIDE HEMS	5" TOTAL	NONE
TOP	2 × POCKET + 2 × HEADING (IF USED)	2 × POCKET + 2 × HEADING (IF USED)

ARCHED VALANCE STEP-BY-STEP

1 Choose and prepare face fabric and lining, joining fabric widths as described (see pages 21–23). Press seams open.

2 With wrong sides together, center and pin lining to face fabric, aligning top and bottom raw edges.

3 On right side of face fabric, measure from upper edge a distance equal to top allowance (2 times pocket plus 2 times heading, if used). Mark with pins every 4 inches across valance to make finished-length line.

4 Draw a paper pattern ½ inch longer than finished length and half the finished width of valance. Divide vertically into fourths.

From top edge, measure and mark shortest point plus ½ inch for hem allowance (10½ inches in example) on line for center of valance; mark longest point plus ½ inch (18½ inches in example) on line for side of valance. Subtract short distance from long and divide by 4 for increment. Measure and mark depth of returns.

Add increment to dimension at center line. At next vertical line, mark that distance from top edge with a standing pin. Continue adding increment to previous distance and pinning at vertical lines. Then move the three pins up to strike a gentle arc, moving the middle pin up most. Mark the curve.

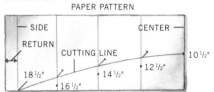

PAPER PATTERN

5 Cut out pattern and lay on half of valance, placing top edge of pattern on finished-length line; mark curved cutting line. Flip pattern and mark other half of valance. Cut face fabric and lining on line. Remove pins.

6 *For a same-fabric facing* (see page 95), stitch facing to lower edge of lining. *For trim* (see page 95), apply to lower edge of face fabric.

7 Pin the lower edges of face fabric and lining right sides together. Stitch, making a ½-inch seam; trim and clip the seam allowances. Turn right side out and press the lower edge. Trim lining so upper edge meets pin-marked finished-length line.

8 For side hems, turn face fabric 2½ inches to the wrong side and press. Turn raw edge in to meet pressed fold and press again. Blindhem by machine or hand-slipstitch hem to lining only.

9 Follow steps 5–6, "Rod-pocket valance," page 91, to finish valance.

tapered valance

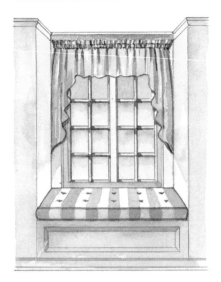

This easy-to-make, gathered valance cascades down the sides of a window, framing the view. It uses a minimum of fabric. A contrast lining looks especially nice on a longer valance.

When calculating the yardage, allow a full width for each tapered side panel and another full width (or more for especially wide windows) for the center portion. Fullness is 3 times the finished width.

Make the center panel 12 to 18 inches long. Tapered valances look best when the side panels are either one-third or two-thirds longer than the center panel.

Use the same calculations as "Arched valance," page 93, and follow steps 1–3. Refer to step 4 to make a paper pattern. On the center line, measure and mark finished length at center plus ½ inch from pin-marked finished-length line.

Repeat for inner corner where center and side widths meet. Draw a line connecting the two points. At end, measure and mark outer finished-length line plus ½ inch. Measure and mark depth of returns.

Draw a line from inner corner to return, rounding corners, for the lower edge of the valance.

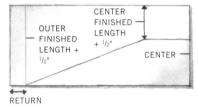

PAPER PATTERN

OUTER FINISHED LENGTH + ½"

CENTER FINISHED LENGTH + ½"

CENTER

RETURN

To complete the valance, follow steps 5–9, "Arched valance," page 93.

scalloped valance

A gently undulating lower hem sets this valance style apart from other shaped valances.

For most fabrics, a fullness of 3 times the finished width is best. The finished length is based on the longest points at the sides. For a scalloped valance over traversing draperies or stationary side panels, the sides and center are often the same length. For a valance over blinds, a shade, or café curtains, the sides are often longer.

Follow the same length guidelines as for a tapered valance center panel (see at left); typically, the difference between the shortest and longest points is 5 inches.

Use the same allowances and follow the same basic instructions as for an "Arched valance" (see page 93), with the following adjustments to the paper pattern:

For a valance with sides and center at same length, mark finished length plus ½ inch at side and center lines; connect with a horizontal line. Mark shortest length plus ½ inch at third (middle) line; draw a horizontal line through point across pattern. Add another horizontal line midway between; at remaining vertical lines, mark points where vertical lines intersect middle horizontal line. Connect points in a gentle curve. Measure and mark depth of returns. Cut out pattern.

PAPER PATTERN

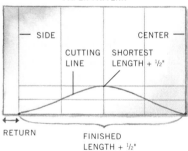

SIDE

CENTER

CUTTING LINE

SHORTEST LENGTH + ½"

RETURN

FINISHED LENGTH + ½"

finishing shaped valances

Sometimes, the lower edges of arched, tapered, and scalloped valances may reveal a bit of the lining from the front. If you wish to hide or disguise the lining, you have several options.

One easy solution is to line the valance with a contrast fabric. Or you can add a deep ruffle or narrow piping to the lower edge. Still another approach is to stitch a same-fabric facing to the lower edge of the lining.

You can also topstitch a contrast band to a scalloped valance, but this trim is tricky to apply and adds bulk.

RUFFLES

To make a folded ruffle, see "Decorative edgings," pages 42–43. Cut ruffle strips on the crosswise grain for the most economical use of fabric.

1 With raw edges aligned, pin ruffle to lower edge of face fabric, aligning ends of ruffle with side hem folds.

2 Baste, making a ½-inch seam.

FLAT PIPING

For ½-inch flat piping, you'll need a 2-inch-wide strip of bias-cut contrast fabric equal in length to the edge to be trimmed plus one inch. For ¼-inch piping, make the strip 1½ inches wide. (Bias-cut strips work best on curved edges but require more fabric.) Note that the piping may not hide the lining.

1 Fold strip in half lengthwise, wrong side in; press. At one end, open strip and turn in ½ inch; finger-press.

2 With raw edges aligned, pin piping to lower edge of face fabric, aligning folded end of strip with side hem fold on valance. Making a ½-inch seam, baste to within a few inches of other side. Trim piping ½ inch beyond side hem fold. Turn in ½ inch; finger-press. Finish basting.

SAME-FABRIC FACING

For an arched or scalloped valance, add 2½ inches plus the difference between the longest and shortest points on the valance to the cut length on your work sheet.

1 Cut face fabric to desired shape, using the leftover fabric for the facing.

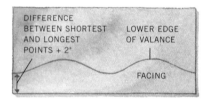

DIFFERENCE BETWEEN SHORTEST AND LONGEST POINTS + 2"

LOWER EDGE OF VALANCE

FACING

2 With right sides together, sew facing piece to bottom edge of lining, aligning straight edges.

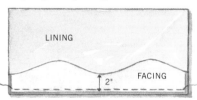

LINING

FACING

2"

3 Press seam toward lining. Recalculate new length of lining needed and trim excess.

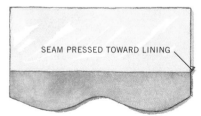

SEAM PRESSED TOWARD LINING

CONTRAST BANDING ON A SCALLOPED VALANCE

You'll need two strips of fabric, each as long as the total valance width. The width of the strips should equal the distance between the high and low points on the lower edge, plus the desired finished width of the banding (typically 1 to 2 inches), plus 1 inch.

1 Lay strips right sides together, aligning raw edges. Placing pattern 1½ inches from each side, cut lower edges. Move pattern up a distance equal to finished width of band plus 1 inch. Mark upper curve and cut long line.

FINISHED WIDTH + 1"

BAND

CUTTING LINE

2 Pin strips together on upper curve and stitch a ½-inch seam. Trim and clip seam allowances. Turn right side out; press edge.

3 Place wrong side of band on right side of valance; baste unfinished edge of band to lower edge of valance. Pin and topstitch finished edge of band to valance. The band will be sandwiched between the face fabric and the lining when the lining is sewn to the bottom edge. On right side, topstitch lower edge of band.

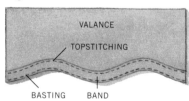

VALANCE

TOPSTITCHING

BASTING

BAND

tab stagecoach valance

This jaunty valance, made in much the same way as a rod-pocket curtain, hangs from a tension rod. Two simple loop tabs hold the valance up at the ends, forming a slightly curved lower edge and tails.

The tension rod mounting makes the valance suitable for a narrow window only. For a series of narrow windows, make several valances.

A self-lining prevents the wrong side of the valance from showing when the lower edge is folded up on itself.

CHOOSING FABRIC. Select a firmly woven fabric that will hold its shape, such as sailcloth or duck. Patterned fabric may show through if the fabric is thin; to test, hold two layers of the fabric up to the light to see the effect.

A striped fabric is ideal because the stripes line up on the front and back. With a striped fabric, consider running the stripes vertically on the valance and horizontally on the tabs.

CALCULATING YARDAGE. Total width equals the width of the window opening, less $1/4$ inch, plus 1 inch for two $1/2$-inch side hems, plus 2 inches for ease pleats. Cut length is equal to 2 times the finished length (12 to 14 inches is a good range for finished length), plus 2 times the pocket size (see the top chart on page 46), plus a 1-inch ravel allowance.

For tabs, you'll need two strips of fabric, each twice the desired finished width ($1^1/2$ to 2 inches, depending on the width of the valance), plus 1 inch for two $1/2$-inch seam allowances. The cut length of each strip is 2 times the finished length.

TAB STAGECOACH VALANCE STEP-BY-STEP

1 Choose and prepare fabric (see pages 21–23).

2 On right side of fabric, measure from lower edge a distance equal to 2 times finished length and mark with pins every 4 inches across valance width. Then measure and mark 2 times pocket size above finished-length line. Trim ravel allowance.

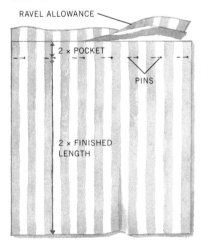

3 Fold panel right side in, so lower raw edge is on pin-marked finished-length line.

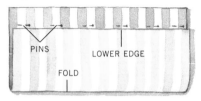

4 Pin and stitch side edges together, making $1/2$-inch seams. Clip at corners.

5 Turn right side out and press edges. Fold down top edge, wrong side in, on finished-length line; press. Turn raw edge in to meet pressed fold and press again. Stitch close to second fold.

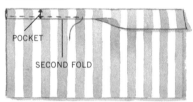

6 For tabs, cut two strips to desired dimensions. Fold each strip in half, right side in, and pin. Stitch, making a $1/2$-inch seam. Turn right side out and press, centering seam at back. Overlap ends and pin.

7 Slip rod through pocket of valance. Pinch 1-inch-deep pleats at the points where the tabs will be placed and slipstitch. This prevents the tails from swinging into the window too far.

8 Fold up valance, and slip tabs over pleats to check length. Adjust length to your liking and repin. Remove tabs and slipstitch the ends. Replace tabs on valance, positioning the stitched ends on wrong side near the top so they do not show.

rolled stagecoach valance

This self-lined valance is rolled up and tied in the center. It can be stapled to a 1½-inch board for an inside or outside mount or used on a tension rod for an inside mount. Use this valance only on a narrow window.

Yardage calculations are similar to the tab stagecoach valance, except that you allow extra length for the roll. Before you buy the fabric, unroll and fold the fabric 20 inches over itself; roll up. Experiment until you arrive at a pleasing roll; then measure the fabric and add to the visible length to arrive at the finished length.

Fabric ties or ribbons can be used as the carrier. The carrier gets stapled to the top of the board, or it is sewn into the rod pocket and wrapped around to the back of the tension rod. Add a bow to the bottom of the carrier.

These stationary valances are shortened versions of Roman, balloon, and cloud shades.

Refer to the instructions for "Flat Roman shade," page 71, "Balloon shade," page 78, and "Cloud shade," page 81.

Typically, shade-style valances are from 20 to 25 inches long. If rings are sewn to the back, the cords are adjusted for proper tension and tied to each screw eye.

Many times, it is not necessary to sew on rings. Simply whipstitch the folds together where rings would have been placed and eliminate the cords.

When making a cloud valance, substitute a rod pocket for the shirring tape at the top edge and gather the fabric on a rod.

A tailed Roman shade is made when the outer rows of rings at the sides are left off.

TAILED ROMAN SHADE VALANCE

BALLOON SHADE VALANCE

CLOUD SHADE VALANCE

pleated valances

A pleated valance sports deep inverted pleats for a tailored look.

When you make the pleats and the spaces between them the same size, you create a classic box-pleated valance. If the pleats are more widely spaced, it's called a kick-pleated valance. Construction is basically the same for both types.

PLANNING. Pleated valances are board-mounted; see the hardware information on page 90 for the board sizes. The return size is equal to the width of the board.

It's best to try to hide seams within the pleats. To do this, you must add up spaces and pleats from one end to see where seams will occur and then adjust the seams as necessary.

Start by choosing space and pleat sizes. A good pleat width is 6 inches (12 inches before being pleated); space width can vary from 6 inches, for a classic box-pleated valance, up to the usable width of the fabric less the pleat size, for a kick-pleated one.

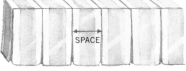

BOX-PLEATED VALANCE

KICK-PLEATED VALANCE

Full pleats are usually placed at each corner, with half the pleat on the front and half on the return. If your return is less than half a pleat wide, place a half-pleat, rather than a full one, at each end.

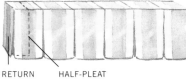

RETURN   HALF-PLEAT

See the valance guidelines on page 90 to choose the finished length, with the following considerations: On a box-pleated valance, the width of the spaces should be less than the finished length of the valance; otherwise, the pleats will appear too square. On a kick-pleated valance, with few pleats, the spaces will be much wider than the valance length.

Once you decide on pleat and space sizes, make a sketch of your valance. For a classic box-pleated style, start adding up pleats and spaces from one end of the valance, beginning with the $1\frac{1}{4}$-inch side hem and the return. When you reach your usable-width figure (52 inches in this example), that's where the first seam will occur. If you're lucky, the seam will fall within a pleat and be hidden.

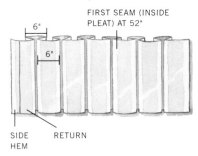

If the seam falls in a space, back up and plan to join widths so the seam falls within the previous pleat.

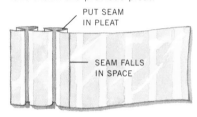

Continue adding spaces and pleats, adjusting seams as necessary and noting their positions on your sketch so you can join widths accurately.

For a kick-pleated valance, follow the same approach. If a seam falls in the first space, you'll need to split a width and seam half to the left side. Shift the fabric to make that seam fall in the first pleat.

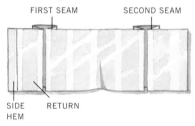

CHOOSING FABRIC. Select fabric with enough body both to form a crisp pleat and to hold its shape between pleats.

It's easiest to use an unpatterned fabric for a pleated valance. With patterned fabric, choose a space size that allows the major motifs to be centered in the spaces. Make sure there's enough fabric between horizontal repeats to make the pleats.

CALCULATING YARDAGE. For either valance, follow these steps:

1 Measure your window and fill in the window treatment work sheet (see pages 16–18) to arrive at board size.

2 Divide the space size into the board size to arrive at the number of spaces. If the result is a fraction, round off to a whole number.

3 Divide number of spaces into board size to get exact space size.

4 Add returns to board size to get finished width.

5 Instead of filling in fullness on work sheet, multiply exact pleat size by number of pleats (one more than number of spaces; but if you have a half-pleat at each corner, number of pleats is same as number of spaces). Add this figure to finished width. Add side hems for total width. Divide by usable width and round up to next whole number for number of widths needed. Add one more width, to provide the play you'll need to hide the seams.

Use the following allowances in your calculations:

	FABRIC	LINING
LOWER HEMS	3"	1½"
SIDE HEMS	5"	NONE
TOP	3"	3"

PLEATED VALANCES STEP-BY-STEP

1 Choose and prepare face fabric and lining (see pages 21–23). Join fabric widths, trimming as necessary to make seams fall as desired. (Don't cut your widths to measurements on sketch, as each seam requires a ½-inch seam allowance). Press seams open.

2 Follow step 2, "Rod-pocket valance," page 91, to stitch lower hem.

3 On right side of face fabric, measure from lower edge a distance equal to finished length and mark with a fabric marker across valance. Measure and mark 3 inches above finished-length line on face fabric and lining. Trim ravel allowance.

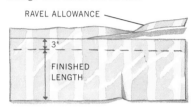

4 With face fabric right side up, measure 1¼-inch double side hems (2½ inches on each side) plus return at one end and pin vertically on finished-length line to mark start of first pleat or half-pleat. Pin same distance on lower edge. Measure and pin first pleat (12 inches for full pleat in example) and first space (6 inches in example).

Continue measuring and pinning pleats and spaces across valance, making sure seams fall within pleats and ending at other return.

Last pleat should fall just before return.

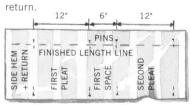

5 Bring pins together so pleats form a flattened loop on back and folds "kiss" on front.

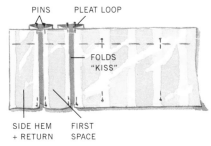

PINS   PLEAT LOOP

FOLDS "KISS"

SIDE HEM + RETURN   FIRST SPACE

On front and back, pin layers together where pleats form folds.

6 For side hems, turn face fabric 2½ inches to the wrong side and press. Turn raw edge in to meet pressed fold and press again. Fold corners diagonally to form miter. Blindhem by machine or hand-slipstitch hem to lining only.

7 Follow first part of step 15, "Flat Roman shade," page 73, to cover mounting board.

8 On right side of valance, measure and cut top allowance ¼ inch less than width of board. Fold along finished-length line and press. Also press pleats in place above finished-length line. Serge or zigzag the top raw edge, joining face fabric and lining.

9 Position valance right side up over board so finished-length fold aligns with top front edge of board and pleats are at corners. Staple top allowance to board; fold and staple returns.

10 Follow directions for an outside mount in step 21, "Flat Roman shade," page 73, to install valance. Support with angle irons every 40 inches.

pleat variations

Interesting effects can be achieved by varying the width and depth of the pleats, spacing pleats farther apart, adding curves to the bottom of spaces, forming box pleats on the outside of the valance, double- or triple-stacking the pleats, or adding tails.

BENTON

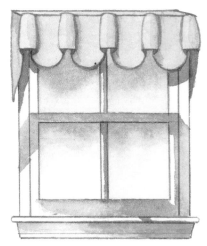

IMPERIAL

CANTERBURY

PALAIS

SAXONY

bandanna valance

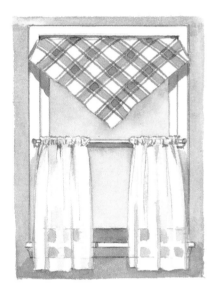

This easy-to-make valance, sometimes called a handkerchief valance, is a simple square or diamond shape lined to the edge in contrasting or self-fabric and attached to a rod by means of a hidden rod pocket. For a fun look, try using plaid tablecloths or large bandannas instead of fabric yardage.

PLANNING. This valance can be made with the front triangle lower and hiding the back or reversed so that the edges of the back triangle are an accent. The placement of the rod pocket determines the look. Because the rod pocket is applied off-center, the ends of the valance hang in short tails.

The best rod to use is a 1³/₈-inch-diameter pole; use it with or without finials.

The length of the valance or point is optional, depending on the look that you want and the amount of view desired. The wider the window and the squarer the shape, the more window is covered.

It is best to keep the width of the finished bandanna valance less than the width of your fabric so that there are no seams in the diamond. The maximum width of the window for this valance style is 42 inches.

CALCULATING YARDAGE. Measure your window and fill in the window treatment work sheet (see pages 16–18). The width from point to point is the bracket-to-bracket measurement plus at least 8 inches (4-inch tails on each side). The length from point to point is the distance from the top of the rod to the bottom point in front times 2.

Cut a piece of fabric and lining 2 inches wider and longer than the point-to-point measurements.

BANDANNA VALANCE STEP-BY-STEP

1 Make a paper pattern for one-half of the length of the finished valance. Draw a horizontal line the total width of the valance at the center. From the center point of the horizontal line, draw a vertical line for one-half of the finished length of the valance. Draw diagonal lines joining the two end points to the bottom of the vertical line. Cut out the pattern.

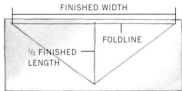

2 Place the face fabric and lining right sides together. Pin the pattern on the fabric and lining and draw around the diagonal edges. Fold the pattern up on the horizontal foldline and draw around the diagonal edges again to complete the total length. Add ¹/₂-inch seam allowances on all sides.

3 With right sides together, stitch around all sides, leaving an opening for turning. Trim corners, turn right side out, and press. Slipstitch opening.

4 With a chalk marker, draw center horizontal line on lining. Measure and mark 1¹/₂ inches to one side of center line and draw a parallel line.

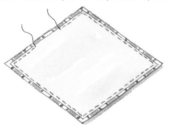

5 Cut a strip of lining fabric wide enough to form a rod pocket (see page 46) plus 1 inch and the length of the bracket-to-bracket measurement plus 1 inch.

6 Press under ¹/₂-inch seam allowances on all sides of strip. Center strip on lining side of valance, matching one edge with second parallel line; edgestitch. Edgestitch other long side, leaving ends open.

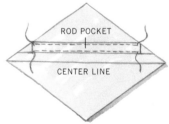

7 Slip a rod into the rod pocket on the back of the valance. Mount rod in the brackets.

Bandanna-style overlays with button accents completely change the look of a padded straight cornice. Mounting the cornice well above the window opening allows the shutters to be opened and closed to regulate the light and makes the windows appear much longer.

LEFT: Just a slight alteration in the shape of the bottom edge adds interest to a simple cornice. The new shape provides a background on which to use an historic fabric like this scenic toile.

BELOW: A fabric with a vertical repeat makes a shaped cornice, especially one as dramatically long as this one, more interesting. There is usually no limit to how long a cornice can be as long as it is amply supported.

how to make cornices

A fabric-covered wood cornice mounted over curtains, draperies, or a shade neatly frames a window and adds architectural interest to a room. A cornice is practical, too—it hides the heading and the hardware at the top of the undertreatment and blocks cold drafts.

You make a scalloped cornice in much the same way that you make a straight cornice; where steps differ, special instructions for the scalloped version are given.

tools and supplies

To make a straight or scalloped welted cornice, you will need the following supplies from a lumberyard: 1-inch No. 2 kiln-dried pine (the width and length depend on the dimensions of your cornice) and $^3/_8$-inch interior fir plywood (the amount depends on the cornice dimensions).

You'll need a saber saw or handsaw, cement-coated box nails, plain pattern paper (for scalloped cornice only), white or craft glue, a paintbrush, scissors, C-clamps, a staple gun, angle irons, and fasteners.

Additional supplies include 8-ounce bonded Dacron batting (enough to wrap around the legs and face board, plus 1 inch on all edges); pushpins; fabric for the cornice, welt, and lining; upholstery tack strips; $^3/_8$-inch cord; and gimp.

planning your cornice

Measure the width of your window from trim to trim. Then decide how far to extend the cornice on either side. The top board must be a minimum of $1^1/_2$ inches longer than the window width or treatment cornice will cover.

The recommended minimum distance above the opening is 8 inches;

the recommended distance into the window opening is 4 inches. If you're running a patterned fabric vertically, the vertical repeat (see page 19) must fit within the desired cornice height.

On a scalloped cornice, the difference between the short and long points should be at least 3 inches. The short points must cover the heading of any undertreatment.

The width of the horizontal board on top depends on what will hang underneath. For an inside-mounted treatment, such as miniblinds or a shade, the top board can be $3^1/_2$ inches wide. But if the cornice will top an outside-mounted treatment, make the top board at least $5^1/_2$ inches wide.

The boards that form the legs are the same width as the top board. Their length is equal to the desired height of the cornice minus $^3/_4$ inch. The plywood face board needs to be as long as the top board; its width is equal to the length of the legs, plus $^3/_4$ inch.

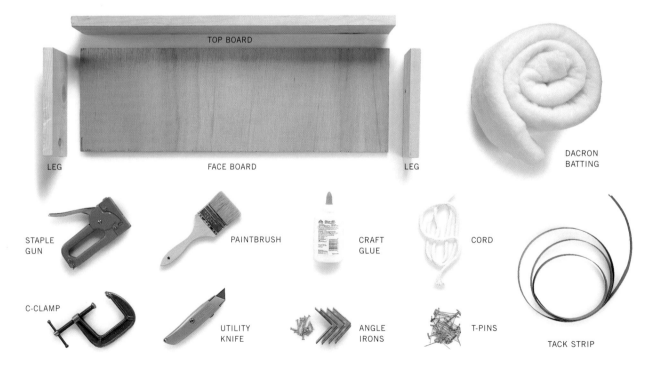

TOP BOARD

LEG

FACE BOARD

LEG

DACRON BATTING

STAPLE GUN

PAINTBRUSH

CRAFT GLUE

CORD

C-CLAMP

UTILITY KNIFE

ANGLE IRONS

T-PINS

TACK STRIP

The tools and supplies necessary for making a cornice are available in a variety of places: lumberyards, hardware stores, craft supply stores, and outlets for sewing supplies.

cornices

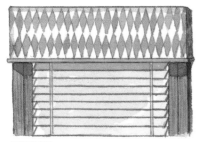

STRAIGHT

SCALLOPED

For a simple, tailored top treatment, make a cornice with a straight lower edge. A scalloped cornice creates a softer look. Select a firmly woven fabric that won't lose its shape.

CALCULATING YARDAGE. If possible, railroad fabric (run selvages parallel to floor) to avoid seams. Most patterned fabric must be run vertically.

Add together long dimension of cornice, returns (depth of legs), and 6 inches for wrapping fabric around legs.

For railroaded fabric, divide by 36 to get yards needed (fabric will be wide enough to cover cornice height).

For fabric run vertically, divide by usable fabric width (less selvages and seams) for number of widths needed. The cut length is equal to the height of the cornice plus 6 inches. To figure repeat cut length for patterned fabric, see page 20. Multiply cut length (or repeat cut length) by number of widths; divide by 36 for yards needed.

Railroad the lining, figuring it as you would face fabric.

Add extra fabric for same-fabric or contrast welt (see step 15, page 106, to determine the length).

CORNICES STEP-BY-STEP

1 Using 1-by lumber for top board and legs and plywood for face board, measure and cut boards to your specifications. Make cuts precise; ends of all boards must be perfectly square.

2 *For a straight cornice,* continue to step 3. *For a scalloped cornice,* make a paper pattern, using a sheet of paper equal to half the long dimension of cornice and deep enough to accommodate short and long points.

Draw half of design, cut out, and tape to face board. Mark outline; flip pattern and mark other half. Cut face board on marked line.

3 Lay out the boards. Start nails for legs at ends of top board. Glue legs to underside of board at ends; finish nailing. Apply glue to front edge of top board and legs. Lay face board over frame.

Using nails, tack face board to top board at corners; tack to legs, pulling legs out to straighten, if necessary. Finish nailing. Measure and mark vertical line at midpoint on face board.

4 Lay cornice, face board up, on sawhorses. On batting, mark midpoint at top and bottom. Dilute glue with water to consistency of heavy cream and brush onto face board. Lay batting on top, aligning marks on board and batting, Let dry.

5 Brush glue on legs; wrap batting around legs, securing on inside of legs with pushpins until glue is dry. Trim batting even with the top, lower, and back edges.

6 *For fabric run vertically,* join widths, as described on page 23; press seams toward center. To avoid a center seam on an even number of widths, cut off half a width and seam to opposite side.

7 Center fabric, right side up, on face board. Smooth over top board; measure and mark fabric 3 inches beyond top front edge. Remove fabric, mark line, and cut on line.

8 Hang cornice, top board up, over sawhorses. On top board, measure and mark a line 2 inches from front edge.

9 Center fabric, wrong side up, on top board so edge of fabric is at marked line and fabric is toward back. Starting at midpoint of top board, lay a tack strip over fabric, aligning edge with raw edge of fabric. Staple strip.

Continue stapling, placing staples 3½ inches apart and adding strips as needed, to within 1 inch of ends of cornice; trim ends.

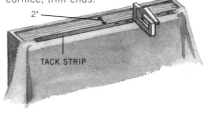

TACK STRIP

10 Flip fabric forward; if any staple has pulled a thread, remove and restaple. Smooth fabric down face board and up underneath. Roll cornice back so top board is down. Clamp to sawhorses.

11 *On a straight cornice,* pull fabric taut at midpoint of face board and, keeping grain straight, wrap around bottom of face board. Staple to inside about 1½ inches from edge, placing staples about 6 inches apart. (Staples are temporary.)

On a scalloped cornice, pull fabric taut and staple at longest point or points. (Staples are temporary.)

For either cornice, pull fabric around legs and staple to inside in several places.

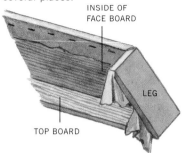

INSIDE OF FACE BOARD

LEG

TOP BOARD

12 Starting at midpoint of face board on a straight cornice or at long points on a scalloped cornice, remove a temporary staple. Pull fabric taut enough to see edge of board, and staple about 1$\frac{1}{2}$ inches from edge.

On a straight cornice, continue removing temporary staples, one at a time, pulling fabric taut, and restapling; keep grain straight and place staples about $\frac{1}{2}$ inch apart. Staple to within 4 inches of ends.

On a scalloped cornice, remove temporary staples, one at a time, pull fabric taut, and restaple. Cut into fabric at curves almost to front edge of face board. Pull each flap of fabric taut and staple to inside. If curve meets a straight edge, fold fabric carefully and staple.

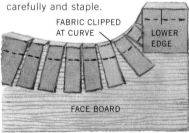

FABRIC CLIPPED AT CURVE

LOWER EDGE

FACE BOARD

13 Restaple legs in same manner, stapling fabric to inside. Roll cornice so top board is up. Fold fabric at top corners, forming miters; staple to top board. Trim close to staples.

14 Roll cornice so top board is down. At corners, cut fabric to inside edge of face board; staple up to inside corners.

Smooth fabric up outside of legs, across bottom, and to inside. At corners and back of legs, neatly fold fabric under; staple to inside. Trim fabric on inside of face board and legs close to staples.

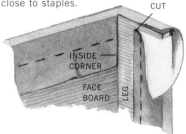

CUT

INSIDE CORNER

FACE BOARD

LEG

15 Measure, mark, and cut enough 6-inch-wide strips of bias fabric to cover lower edge of face board and legs and, if making same-fabric welt, to extend up back edge of each leg, plus 2 inches for each end plus 6 inches for each seam. Seam strips on bias; trim seam allowances and press open.

Lay cord on wrong side of strip. Fold strip over cord, making one seam allowance 1$\frac{1}{2}$ inches wider than the other. Stitch close to cord.

16 Starting at one end of face board and leaving enough welt to cover adjoining leg and, for same-fabric welt, back of leg, lay welt on front edge of face board with narrower seam allowance underneath. Trim tack strips to $\frac{3}{8}$ inch. Miter one end of a tack strip; open welt and lay strip on top.

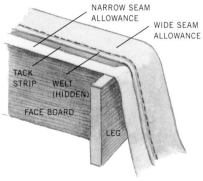

NARROW SEAM ALLOWANCE

WIDE SEAM ALLOWANCE

TACK STRIP

WELT (HIDDEN)

FACE BOARD

LEG

Push tack strip against welt stitching; at same time, gently pull on bottom seam allowance so stitching is drawn slightly under strip.

17 Staple tack strip to edge of face board, placing staples about 1 inch apart and adding strips as needed. *For a scalloped cornice,* clip welt seam allowances to within $\frac{1}{2}$ inch of welt stitching and stretch welt slightly around curves.

At opposite corner, miter tack strip.

18 Miter another tack strip and use to staple welt along bottom of leg. Flatten and staple excess fabric in corner.

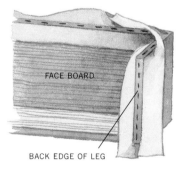

FACE BOARD

LEG

EXCESS FABRIC

For same-fabric welt, continue stapling strip and welt up back of leg; trim strip even with edge.

For contrast welt, trim strip at back corner of leg. Repeat on other leg.

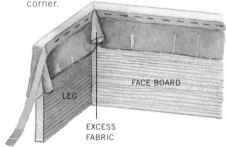

FACE BOARD

BACK EDGE OF LEG

Trim narrower welt seam allowance close to tack strip.

19 Roll cornice so top board is up. Cut welt 1½ inches beyond end of tack strip. Rip out stitching and cut cord even with top board.

For same-fabric welt, fold fabric strip and staple to top board.

For contrast welt, fold strip and staple to inside of leg.

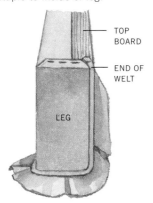

TOP BOARD

END OF WELT

LEG

20 Roll cornice so top board is down. Starting on face board, gently pull wider welt seam allowance down and staple just below previous staples, placing staples 1 inch apart.

At inside corners, cut into seam allowance as before, forming a fabric flap. Miter seam allowance at back edge of leg and staple. Fold fabric flap down and staple to inside corner.

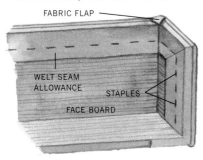

FABRIC FLAP

WELT SEAM ALLOWANCE

STAPLES

FACE BOARD

21 Roll cornice so top board is up. Center lining over top board with fabric toward front and raw edge of lining aligned with front edge of first tack strip (hidden).

Lay another strip on lining so edge of strip is snug against first strip; staple strip along length. Trim ends of strip.

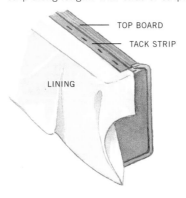

TOP BOARD

TACK STRIP

LINING

22 Flip lining to back, and trim even with each end of top board. At back edge, cut lining at an angle so you can fold lining under. Turn under raw edge of lining and staple to top board.

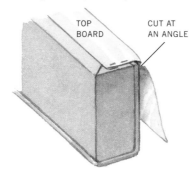

TOP BOARD

CUT AT AN ANGLE

23 Roll cornice so top board is down. Smooth lining to inside and staple long edge where top board meets face board. At inside leg, fold lining over itself and cut ½ inch beyond where leg meets top board; fold lining under and staple to underside of top board.

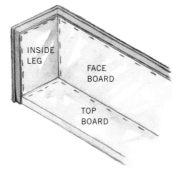

INSIDE LEG

FACE BOARD

TOP BOARD

24 Staple inside edge where face board meets leg. Smooth fabric over inside of leg. Trim remaining flap of fabric to ½ inch; turn under and staple to inside of leg.

25 Trim lining 1 inch beyond back edge of leg; turn under and staple leg. Repeat on other leg.

26 Staple lining to lower edge of cornice, just above previous staples. Trim close to staples. Glue gimp over raw edges.

27 Follow directions for an outside mount in step 21, "Flat Roman shade," page 73, to install cornice. Support with angle irons every 40 inches.

shape variations

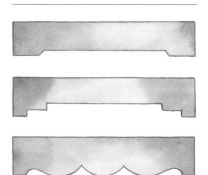

Cornice board shapes can be cut to coordinate with the architecture of your home, the style of your furnishings, or other design details.

Use the construction methods described in "Scalloped valance," page 94. Proportions vary, but rarely are the longest points of a valance more than 18 inches and the shortest less than 12 inches.

OPPOSITE TOP: An extra-long scarf swag with a knot in the center beautifully frames an even more beautiful view. A light filmy fabric is just the right touch.

OPPOSITE BOTTOM: A cutout swag and cascade hung asymmetrically soften the edges of this imposing window with its dramatic city view. The soft folds of the swag contrast with the geometry of the windowpanes.

The cascades in this cutout swag and cascade treatment become elegant, puddled side panels. The precise curves of the swags repeat the scalloped edge of the bedspread, and the white fabrics contrast nicely with the blue trim.

LEFT: The swag and cascade is a formal treatment often used in classically styled rooms such as this one. The lining is an important element that is revealed as the fabric cascades down the sides of the window.

BELOW: To maximize the view out of this small window, deliberately shallow double "kissing" swags are used, and matching cascades with narrow pleats stop at the middle of the window.

ABOVE: This dramatic window treatment is a variation of a cutout swag and cascade without the space for the cutout. An extra fullness of a sheer fabric is draped over a decorative rod in uneven swags and asymmetric cascades. A certain imperfection is achieved.

LEFT: Reversing the usual order can have interesting results. The "cascades" in this treatment are full-length panels mounted over rather under the traditional single swag. Lace panels, usually hung by the window glass to filter the light, are placed on top of the silk panels and face out into the room.

ABOVE: Narrow scarf swags in
classic blue and white play up the
large traditionally paned windows
and let abundant light into the
Early American–styled living room.

RIGHT: Hung from an oversized wood
rod, cutout swags in two fabrics
alternate across the top of these corner
windows and are partnered with long
cascades that reach to the bottom edge
of the window. A thick fringe outlines
the curving edges of the treatment.

LEFT: Striped side panels and a wide sleeve-covered rod create a backdrop for a lively floral print cutout swag, short cascades, and center jabot. This multilayered treatment draws the eye to the top of the window; the shutters adjust for light and privacy.

BELOW: Sometimes embellishments make the treatment. Here, soft jabots, topped with choux add exclamation points to the mixed fabric swags and cascades that decorate the corner windows of this dining room.

Whether casual or formal, swags and cascades impart a look of timeless beauty. Some styles are simple to make; others are more difficult.

Simply put, swags are top treatments that are board-mounted, placed in swag holders, or wrapped around a pole. They're almost always paired with cascades or other side treatments, such as tied-back curtains or straight panels.

You can make swags in a variety of styles. Traditional swags possess a simplicity that belies their construction. What appear to be swatches of fabric nonchalantly draped over boards are, in fact, structured, precise window treatments. Closely related are cutout swags, which also hang on the bias but are open at the top.

Cascades are pleated side panels that flank traditional or cutout swags. Because all lines are straight, they're simple to make.

If you like the look of swags and cascades but prefer an easier project, consider a running swag. Made from one length of fabric, a running swag offers a less structured look than traditional swags and cascades.

Rosettes, choux, and cocards (see pages 126–127) are flowerlike accessories used to embellish swags and cascades.

swag hardware

Traditional swags and cascades are mounted on boards (shown below). For swags used with cascades, a 3$\frac{1}{2}$-inch board is best. For swags used over additional treatments, measure the width needed and choose a board that will clear both the heading and the hardware beneath it.

Cutout swags are attached to decorative rods with hook-and-loop fastener tape. You can use a decorative traverse rod without the rings; the flat back on these rods makes it easy to attach the tape. Or attach the fastener tape to a pole 1$\frac{3}{8}$ inches or larger in diameter.

Running swags can hang from decorative poles, tulip-shaped or circular swag holders, medallion or scarf swag holders, or swag rings. Running swags with knots or ties are mounted on boards.

Many holdbacks (see page 55) also work as swag holders.

choosing fabric

Since a successful swag depends on the fabric's draping qualities, make sure your fabric is soft enough to drape yet firm enough to form and retain folds.

To test a fabric's draping qualities, unroll several yards and fold the cut edge to one selvage. Grasp two diagonally opposite corners and hold the fabric up to see how the fold falls. If it drapes nicely, the fabric will make softly rounded swags. If the fold breaks rather than drapes, you can still use the fabric, but you'll have to work harder to form the pleats. If a fabric doesn't have enough body, try draping the fabric with lining.

Some running swags can be made from firmly woven fabrics, such as chintz, since the hardware determines the swag's form. Wrapped swags lend themselves to sateen and other soft fabrics. Avoid fabrics with obvious one-way patterns because the cascades will run in opposite directions.

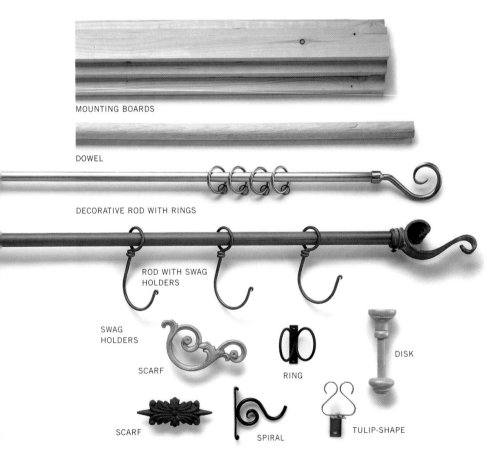

MOUNTING BOARDS

DOWEL

DECORATIVE ROD WITH RINGS

ROD WITH SWAG HOLDERS

SWAG HOLDERS

SCARF

SCARF

SPIRAL

RING

DISK

TULIP-SHAPE

A selection of swag hardware includes mounting boards, dowels, curtain rods, and swag holders in interesting shapes to coordinate with any decor.

traditional swags and cascades

Making beautiful swags takes time, as well as some creativity. Before you commit to yards of fabric, make a sample swag using the fabric and lining you like to get a feel for how swags are made and what they'll look like.

The swags and cascades in this project are pleated; directions are also given for a version that has soft gathers at the top.

PLANNING TRADITIONAL SWAGS

A swag starts with a square of fabric 6 inches larger than the desired finished width, which can range from 36 to 48 inches, depending on the width of your fabric. Length varies; in general, it will be about one-third the size of the fabric square.

Swags can be used singly or in a series; the number depends on both board size and swag size. Swags often overlap by half the swag width, an arrangement called a classic swag. Swags can also meet, or "kiss."

CLASSIC SWAGS

KISSING SWAGS

Swags are usually installed 8 inches above the top of the window opening or at ceiling height. For a series of swags, the point where the swags cross should reach 2 to 4 inches into the window area.

Typically, swags used with cascades extend 4 to 6 inches beyond the opening, with a portion of each cascade covering the window. If you're planning tied-back side panels, place half the panel on the window. For straight panels, place most of each panel off the window. To plan a swag treatment, complete the following steps:

1 Measure your window width and add extensions (see page 16) to arrive at board size. (In example, the board size is 90 inches.)

2 *For swags that meet,* divide board size by 40 inches (a trail swag width) and round up to next whole number to arrive at number of swags (90 ÷ 40 = 2.25, rounds up to 3). *For overlapping swags,* multiply the board size by 1½, divide by 40, and round up to next whole number (90 x 1½ = 135 ÷ 40 = 3.38, rounds up to 4).

3 Sketch your arrangement, showing full swags and half-swags, if swags overlap. Add number of full and half-swags that you see (1 full swag + 3 half-swags = 2½).

FULL SWAG HALF SWAG HALF SWAG HALF SWAG

4 Divide board size by result in step 3 for actual swag width in inches (90 ÷ 2½ = 36).

CALCULATING YARDAGE. Add 6 inches to the actual finished width to arrive at the cut length of each square. For patterned fabric, figure the repeat cut length following steps 2–3 on page 20. For a single swag, cut only one length; for more than one swag, multiply the cut length or repeat cut length by the number of swags.

Use lining the same width as your fabric; buy the same amount.

SWAG TIPS. When pleating your swag, have a helper stand on the other side of your work area. Otherwise, make and pin pleats one at a time on each side. Either way, you'll need to make adjustments to achieve uniformly rounded folds.

A grid cardboard cutting board is helpful for pleating the swag to the correct finished width.

TRADITIONAL SWAGS STEP-BY-STEP

1 Choose and prepare face fabric and lining (see pages 21–23).

2 Measure, mark, and cut a square of lining equal to finished swag width plus 6 inches (42 inches in example).

3 Fold lining in half diagonally, wrong side in, making a triangle; fold again, bringing first fold almost to side. Finger-press folds.

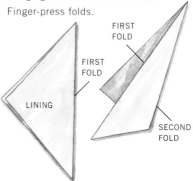

4 Unfold lining, wrong side up, and mark a point on center fold 1 inch longer than side of square (43 inches in example). Also, mark points on intermediate folds ¹/₂ inch longer than side of square (42¹/₂ inches in example). Strike a curve through marks from one corner to the other.

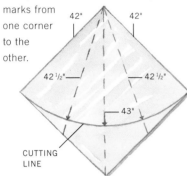

CUTTING LINE

Cut curve. If you've made a sample swag, cut linings for additional swags now, using first piece as a pattern.

5 Position face fabric right side up and determine top point of swag (make sure motifs on patterned fabric are going in right direction). Lay lining over face fabric, right sides together, aligning sides. If fabric is patterned, move lining until repeat is centered as desired.

Pin layers together 1 inch above curve; cut face fabric along curve. Stitch, making a ¹/₂-inch seam.

6 Turn right side out. Understitch through lining and seam allowances only ¹/₈ inch from seam. Press curve, turning ¹/₈ inch of face fabric to lining side.

Pin face fabric and lining together up center.

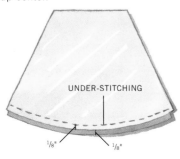

UNDER-STITCHING

¹/₈"   ¹/₈"

7 With face fabric right side up, measure from top point down each side a distance equal to one-third finished swag width (12 inches in example); pin perpendicular to side. Using chalk, mark a horizontal line between pins; mark a dot ³/₄ inch in from edge on each side. Measure and mark another horizontal line 3 inches below first line.

If finished swag width is 42 inches or less, add 1 inch to distance along edge below first marked line and divide by 5. *If finished swag width is 43 inches or more,* add 1 inch to distance and divide by 6. Measure those increments along edge and mark with pins for pleat positions (last pleat will be slightly smaller).

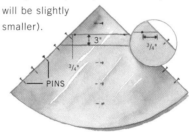

3"
³/₄"
PINS

8 Place swag right side up. Line up top point with center line and place lower horizontal line on front edge of work surface. Pin; let the rest hang free.

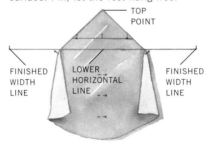

TOP POINT

FINISHED WIDTH LINE

LOWER HORIZONTAL LINE

FINISHED WIDTH LINE

9 On one edge, grasp fabric at second pin and, angling pleat, bring to ³/₄-inch dot; secure with a pushpin. Repeat on other side.

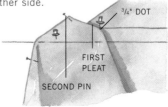

³/₄" DOT
FIRST PLEAT
SECOND PIN

10 Continue making and pinning pleats, keeping spacing even and stair-stepping pleats. Make last pleat so cut edge is parallel to front edge of work surface and the distance across equals the desired swag width. Adjust pleats as necessary.

Working from both sides, coax pleats into rounded folds; adjust and repin as necessary.

FINISHED WIDTH LINE

FINISHED WIDTH LINE

Pin pleats together. Check swag length; if too long, remove anchoring pushpins and move entire swag back from edge, adjusting pleats as needed.

For a gathered swag, unpin pleats, one at a time, and make small tucks; hand-stitch tucks with a long gathering stitch 1¹/₂ inches from edge of work surface. Hem should meet finished width lines.

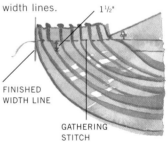

1¹/₂"

FINISHED WIDTH LINE

GATHERING STITCH

11 Mark a line on swag parallel to and 1¹/₂ inches from edge of work surface. Place lower edge of 1-inch masking tape on marked line. Stitch on line through all layers; remove pins. Trim swag along upper edge of tape; remove tape.

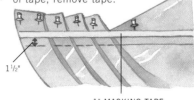

1¹/₂"

1" MASKING TAPE

12 Cut a lining strip 4 inches wide by swag width; have a selvage along one long edge, or finish one edge. With right sides together, pin raw edge of strip to edge of swag. Stitch 1 inch from edge using the previous stitching as a guide.

Wrap strip over edge to the back side of swag. Edgestitch through all layers.

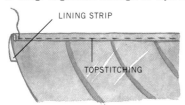

PLANNING CASCADES

Cascades can go over or under a swag.For color and pattern continuity, self-line cascades. But if you want to see another color or pattern from the front where the pleats break, line the cascades with a contrast fabric. Cut a sample cascade from lining or scrap fabric and experiment with length and pleat and space sizes before you cut your face fabric.

Traditional cascades are pleated, though you can gather them to match gathered swags. On a gathered cascade, the inside edge appears scalloped.

Length varies, depending on the look you want to achieve. As a rule, the cascade at its longest point is at least twice as long as the swag.

Where you begin the taper on a cascade is important. The higher the taper, the more lining you'll see. Begin the taper above or several inches below the lowest point on the swag; avoid beginning the taper even with the bottom of the swag.

Each cascade is made from one width of fabric. A typical cascade has a 4-inch leading edge space, four 6-inch pleats alternating with three 2-inch spaces, and a return; finished width is 10 inches, not including the return.

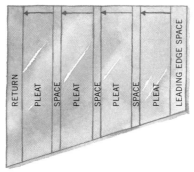

For a narrower cascade, make the pleats 7 inches and the spaces 1 inch for a finished width of 7 inches.

Sketch your cascade and add up the sizes of the pleats and spaces to determine where to trim the fabric width; be sure to add a $1/2$-inch seam allowance on each side.

For a gathered cascade, multiply desired finished width by $2^{1}/_{2}$ and add seam allowances to arrive at cut width.

CALCULATING YARDAGE. Each cascade requires one width of fabric the desired finished length (measured at the longest point), plus 4 inches total for seam allowances and an allowance to go over the top of the mounting board.

Take into account repeats on patterned fabric: cascades look best if a full repeat is at the top, just below where the cascades break over the board. Or you can center one repeat on the cascade, splitting repeats above and below. Don't put a full repeat at the bottom—most of the design will be cut away when the cascade is tapered. Place repeats at the same level on cascades; they won't be mirror images of each other, but the arrangement of the color will be the same.

If your fabric doesn't have a directional pattern and you're making self-lined cascades, you can save fabric by cutting cascades as shown below. You can use the lower portion of fabric to line the opposite cascade.

CASCADES STEP-BY-STEP

1 Lay lining and face fabric right sides together; trim both to finished flat width plus 1 inch. On leading edge of each cascade, measure and mark from top a distance equal to start of taper plus 4 inches. Using a straightedge, draw a line from mark to opposite lower corner. Cut on line.

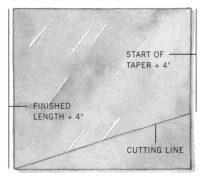

2 Pin lining and face fabric together on all edges except top. Stitch, making a $1/2$-inch seam; trim seam allowances at corners. Turn right side out and lightly press edges. If fabric is heavy, serge or zigzag top raw edges together.

3 Lay cascade on work surface. At return edge, measure and mark the finished-length line; extend the line across the top.

4 *For a pleated cascade,* measure and mark pleats and spaces with pins.

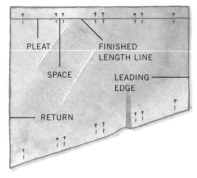

PLEAT
FINISHED LENGTH LINE
SPACE
LEADING EDGE
RETURN

Form pleats, working from return to leading edge. Pin in place at top edge and along finished-length line.

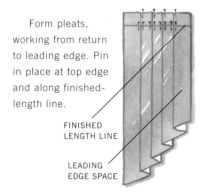

FINISHED LENGTH LINE
LEADING EDGE SPACE

For a gathered cascade, run a long gathering stitch by hand 1½ inches beyond finished-length line. Gather to desired finished width.

5 With right side up, place lower edge of 1-inch masking tape on finished-length line. Stitch pleats or gathers in place along top edge of tape. Measure 1½ inches beyond stitching and mark another line; cut on line. Remove tape.

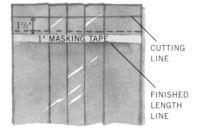

1½"
1" MASKING TAPE
CUTTING LINE
FINISHED LENGTH LINE

Serge or overcast top edge with a wide zigzag stitch, joining face fabric and lining.

MOUNTING TRADITIONAL SWAGS AND CASCADES

Staple traditional swags and cascades to a mounting board. Or, to make removal easier, use hook-and-loop fastener tape.

1 Follow first part of step 15, "Flat Roman shade," page 73, to cover mounting board.

2 Pin the swag or cascade that will appear underneath to the board first, so finished-length line is at front edge of board; check length and adjust if necessary. Repeat for other treatment. Fold cascade at corner for return.

3 Staple cascade to board, placing staples about 2 inches apart.

4 Follow directions for an outside mount in step 21, "Flat Roman shade," page 73, to install. Support with angle irons every 40 inches.

MAKING A JABOT

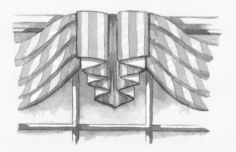

A jabot is a board-mounted decorative transition element used between swags. It can be short or long, self-lined or lined in a contrasting fabric.

On the short jabot, the longest point should be shorter than the swag. Typically, the side taper begins 5 to 8 inches above the longest point, pleats are 6 inches wide, spaces between pleats are 1 inch, and side

spaces are 3 inches. Finished width is 10 inches.

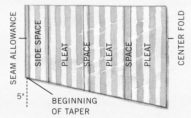

SEAM ALLOWANCE
SIDE SPACE
PLEAT
SPACE
PLEAT
SPACE
PLEAT
CENTER FOLD
5"
BEGINNING OF TAPER

On a longer jabot, side taper begins at longest point of swag or below; finished length varies. Pleats are 6 inches wide, spaces between pleats are 2 inches, and side spaces are 4 inches. Finished width is 16 inches.

1 *Cut the face fabric and lining to finished length plus 4 inches for a ½-inch seam allowance and an allowance to go over the top of the mounting board.*

2 *Place fabric and lining right sides together. Stitch all around, leaving an opening for turning. Turn right side out, press, and slipstitch closed.*

3 *Mark the finished-length line, and mark pleats and spaces at both top and bottom edges.*

4 *Form pleats, working from center to outer edges. Place lower edge of 1-inch masking tape on finished-length line, and stitch pleats in place along top edge of tape. From finished-length line, stitch another line at a distance equal to width of board less ½ inch. Trim ¼ inch beyond stitching.*

5 *Staple jabot to mounting board so the finished-length line is at the front edge of the board.*

cutout swags and cascades

Attached to decorative poles and often combined with sheers, miniblinds, or pleated shades, cutout swags and cascades are a lighter alternative to traditional swags and cascades. The only difference between them is that cutout swags have an open area on top so the rod shows.

Because cutout swags are open at the top, the coverage they provide for an undertreatment is shallow. If you're planning an undertreatment other than cascades, such as floor-length or puddled side panels, be sure to mount the swags so they conceal the undertreatment's heading.

Making cutout swags takes time and a willingness to experiment with fabric. Make a sample first to get a feel for how the swags are made and to see if you like the look.

Because of the way they're attached, cutout swags and cascades are the most difficult to make of all the swag treatments. This project gives instructions for swags and cascades without returns. If you want to cover the gap between the treatment and the window, make them with returns as described on page 122.

PLANNING CUTOUT SWAGS. For guidelines in choosing fabric, see pages 21–23.

Cutout swags appear to flow across the pole; cascades can go behind or over the pole at the ends. The swags shown below overlap each other (in this example, each is 36 inches wide, with a 16-inch cutout and two 10-inch overlaps). The cascades are behind the pole.

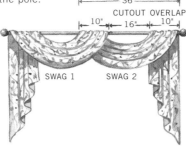

Swags start with a square of fabric 6 inches larger than the desired finished width, which can range from 32 to 48 inches, depending on your fabric's width. The cutout should be between 16 and 20 inches wide. Overlaps are from 8 to 12 inches; 10 inches is standard.

The rod or pole is usually installed 8 inches above the top of the window opening. Extensions for swags used with cascades are typically 4 to 6 inches, allowing a portion of each cascade to cover the window. If you're planning tied-back side panels rather than cascades, place half of each panel on the window and half off. For straight panels, place most of each panel off the window.

Because rods and poles hang from brackets placed near or at the ends, the treatment will cover only the distance from the inside of one bracket to the inside of the other.

To figure the number of swags and their width, complete the following steps. If you want one more swag than this method yields, return to step 3 and refigure, using the new number of swags.

1 Measure your window width and add extensions (see page 16) to arrive at rod or pole size. (In the following example, rod or pole size, from bracket to bracket, is 62 inches.)

2 Divide rod or pole size by a trial swag size of 35 inches, and round off to nearest whole number to arrive at number of swags ($62 \div 35 = 1.8$, rounded to 2).

3 Multiply number of overlaps (one more than number of swags) by a trial overlap size of 10 inches ($3 \times 10 = 30$ inches).

4 Subtract result in step 3 from rod or pole size; divide by number of swags to arrive at cutout size of each swag ($62 - 30 = 32 \div 2 = 16$ inches).

If cutout size is less than 16 inches, reduce trial overlap in step 3 to 9 inches and refigure; if cutout is still less than 16 inches, reduce overlap to 8 inches and refigure. If cutout size is greater than 24 inches, increase overlap to 11 or 12 inches and refigure.

5 To cutout size, add 2 times overlap size to arrive at swag width ($16 + 20 = 36$ inches). Sketch your treatment.

CALCULATING YARDAGE. Calculate yardage for cutout swags in the same way as for traditional swags (see page 115).

SWAG TIPS. It's easier to pleat a swag if you have a helper on one side. If you work alone, make and pin pleats one at a time on each side. Either way, you'll need to adjust pleats and repin a bit to make uniformly rounded folds.

A grid cardboard cutting board is helpful for pleating the swag to the correct finished width.

CUTOUT SWAGS AND CASCADES STEP-BY-STEP

1 Choose and prepare face fabric and lining (see pages 21–23).

2 Follow steps 2–4, "Traditional swags," pages 115–116, to cut lining and lower curve.

3 With lining right side up, measure and mark from top point down each side a distance equal to cutout size plus 3 inches (19 inches in example). Measure and mark from top point down center a distance equal to cutout size plus 2 inches (18 inches in example). Strike a gentle curve from side marks to center mark; cut along curve.

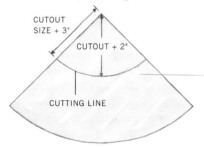

4 Position face fabric right side up and determine top of swag (make sure motifs on patterned fabric are going in right direction). Lay lining over face fabric, right sides together, aligning sides. If fabric is patterned, move lining until repeat is centered as desired.

Pin layers together along curves; cut face fabric along curves. Pin and stitch lower curve only, making a ¹/₂-inch seam.

5 Follow step 6, "Traditional swags," page 116, to understitch lower curve, disregarding instructions to pin swag up center.

Turn right sides together again. Pin and stitch upper curve, making a ¹/₂-inch seam. Turn right side out and press.

6 Measure distance along each side and divide by 5 to arrive at pleat size. If less than 5 inches, divide distance by 4. Measure pleat size incrementally along edges and mark with pins for pleat positions.

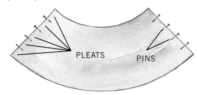

7 Use tape to mark finished swag width (36 inches in example) and midpoint (18 inches) directly on work surface or cutting board. On each side of midpoint, mark half the cutout size (8 inches).

8 At upper curve, turn under 1¹/₂ inches just on sides. On each side, pin first pleat to work surface, angling and aligning with cutout lines. Secure the pleat with pushpins.

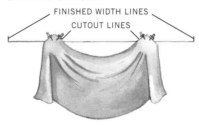

9 Continue making and pinning pleats, keeping spacing even and stair-stepping pleats. Make last pleat so cut edge is parallel to edge of work surface and hem meets finished width lines. Adjust pleats as necessary.

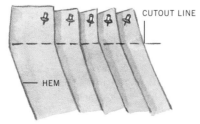

Starting at top and working from both sides, form pleats into rounded folds; adjust and repin as necessary.

Pin pleats together. Check swag length; if too long, remove anchoring pins and move entire swag back from edge, adjusting pleats as needed.

For gathered swag, unpin pleats, one at a time, and make small tucks; using a long gathering stitch, hand-stitch tucks 1¹/₂ inches from work surface edge. Hem should meet finished width marks.

10 *To make cascades,* follow steps 1–4, "Cascades," pages 117–118, disregarding references to returns. With cutout swags, cascades can go over or behind pole. Make finished width equal to size of overlaps (10 inches in example).

11 To determine length of hook-and-loop fastener tape, multiply number of swag overlaps by 2; multiply result by size of each overlap plus 1 inch (in example, 3 x 2 = 6 x 11 = 66 inches).

12 Cut two strips of hook-and-loop fastener tape equal to the overlap size plus 1 inch.

On a rod with a flat back, glue hook (stiff) strips to rod at ends.

On a round pole, have a helper hold pole securely on work surface. Using a board laid against pole as a guide, attach masking tape in a straight line. Align hook strips with masking tape and glue at ends.

For more than one swag, attach other strips at overlap positions.

13 *For a swag or cascade that goes over rod,* proceed to step 14.

For a swag or cascade that goes behind rod, measure distance from bottom of rod to top of hook strip.

On treatment, measure and mark finished-length line; pin perpendicular to line and baste. Measure and mark another line beyond finished-length line at distance just determined. Place top edge of masking tape on top line.

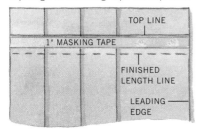

Stitch on top line; trim ¼ inch beyond stitching. Remove masking tape and basting.

14 *For a swag or cascade that goes over rod,* determine distance over rod to bottom of hook strip on back (typically 2½ to 3 inches) by having a helper hold a straightedge vertically behind rod so finished length measurement (16 inches in example) is at top of rod. With a flexible tape measure, measure from bottom of hook strip on back of rod, up and over rod, to bottom of straightedge.

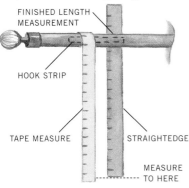

From this figure, subtract finished length of swag or cascade for distance needed beyond finished-length line.

On treatment, mark finished-length line; pin along line and baste. Measure and mark another line beyond finished-length line at distance just determined. Place the top edge of the masking tape on top line.

Stitch on the top line; trim ¼ inch beyond stitching. Remove the tape and the basting.

MOUNTING CUTOUT SWAGS AND CASCADES

Review the arrangement shown on page 119, if used (directions that follow are for that arrangement). A helpful hint in determining which strip to use: hook strips face the wall; loop strips face the room.

For other arrangements, sketch the treatment to help you plan the order of attachment. Swags and cascades should give the illusion of being a continuous piece of fabric. Attach the swags or cascades that go behind the rod before those that go over the rod.

1 Install the rod or pole (see pages 37 and 59).

2 On front of each cascade, sew a loop strip, aligning top of strip with top row of stitching. On back, sew a hook strip.

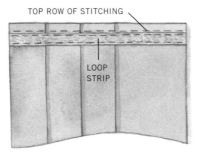

3 On outer overlaps of swags 1 and 2, which go over rod, sew a loop strip to back, aligning the top of strip with row of stitching. Repeat at the center overlap of swag 1.

4 On center overlap of swag 2, which goes behind rod, sew a loop strip to front of swag and a hook strip to back.

5 Attach cascades to rod. At ends, place swags over rod and attach to cascades.

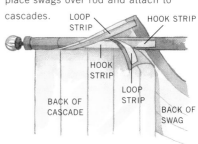

6 At center, attach swag 2 behind rod; lift swag 1 over rod and attach to back of swag 2.

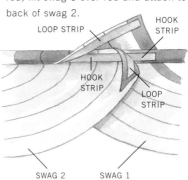

cutout swags and cascades with returns

Returns cover the gap between the window and the treatment at the sides. A notch at the top of each cascade allows the return to attach to the top of the bracket (use metal rather than wood brackets).

CUTOUT SWAGS AND CASCADES WITH RETURNS STEP-BY-STEP

1 Follow steps 1–9, "Cutout swags and cascades," page 120, to make swags.

2 Follow steps 1–4, "Cascades," pages 117–118, to make cascades; return size equals distance from back of bracket to front of rod. Finished width of each cascade, not counting return, should equal size of overlaps (10 inches in example).

3 Make a paper pattern for notch equal to finished width before cutting fabric. Mark return.

On a cascade that goes behind rod, trim top edge of cascade face 1 inch shorter than return portion. Where return begins, cut a V-shaped notch extending into cascade a depth equal to width of hook-and-loop fastener tape.

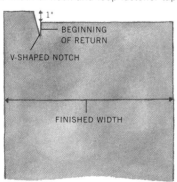

On a cascade that goes over rod, trim top edge of return 1 inch shorter than face. Where return begins, cut a J-shaped notch as deep as circumference of rod plus 2 inches and as wide as rod diameter.

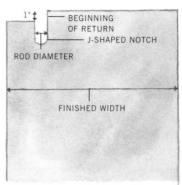

Make a fabric pattern, altering depth of notch if necessary.

4 Follow steps 11–12, "Cutout swags and cascades," page 120, to attach fastener tape to rod.

5 *For a swag that goes behind rod,* follow step 13, "Cutout swags and cascades," pages 120–121.

For a cascade that goes behind rod, measure distance from bottom of rod to top of hook strip (typically 1 to 1½ inches). Mark this distance above the finished-length line and place top edge of masking tape along that line just up to return. On return, place top edge of tape 1 inch above that line.

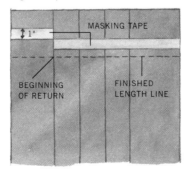

Stitch along top edges of tape; trim fabric ¼ inch beyond stitching. Trim fabric flap where return begins and remove the tape.

6 *For a swag that goes over rod,* follow step 14, "Cutout swags and cascades," page 121.

For a cascade that goes over rod, follow first two paragraphs of step 14, "Cutout swags and cascades," page 121. Measure and mark finished-length line; baste. Measure and mark another line beyond finished-length line at distance just determined. Place top edge of masking tape on top line.

Stitch on top line; trim ¼ inch beyond stitching. Remove tape.

Trim return portion 1 inch shorter than cascade face; serge or overcast top edges together.

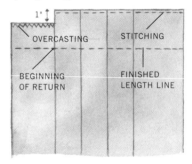

7 Using paper pattern, cut V-shaped or J-shaped notch in returns. Serge or zigzag the edges together, and remove the basting.

8 Follow steps 1–6, "Mounting cutout swags and cascades," page 121, to mount treatments, with these additional considerations for cascades: On a cascade that goes behind rod, loop strips are attached to front of cascade and back of return; on one that goes over rod, loop strips are attached to back of cascade and return; for either, glue a hook strip to top of each bracket.

Running swags offer a less structured look than traditional or cutout swags and cascades. Use them alone to frame a window or combine them with other treatments for a soft effect.

Several different styles are presented here. What makes each distinctive is the method of attachment. A running swag can be pulled through or draped over swag holders, held up by tabs or separate knots, or wrapped around a decorative rod or pole. The basic swag is the same for each style.

PLANNING RUNNING SWAGS. For most swags, two fabric widths are best, unless the window is small; then you can use one fabric width. If your fabric is sheer, consider using three widths.

The following simple swag consists of two widths tapered and seamed to form a tube. A self-lined swag requires two lengths of the same fabric; a contrast-lined swag requires one length each of face fabric and contrast fabric.

Directions for determining the cut length accompany each project. The portion of the swag that becomes the cascades can vary from one-third to two-thirds the window length. Long cascades can be puddled (add 12 inches), avoiding the difficulty of achieving an exact floor length.

If you choose asymmetrical cascades, make sure lengths differ significantly—slight variations just look like mistakes.

1 Measure your window width and add extensions (see page 16). Recommended width for each swag is 35 to 50 inches.

2 For two or more swags, divide rod or board size or distance between holders by desired swag width; round off to nearest whole number to arrive at number of swags.

3 Divide the rod or board size or distance between holders by the number of swags for exact swag size. For number of swag holders, add 1 to the number of swags.

RUNNING SWAGS STEP-BY-STEP

1 Choose and prepare face fabric and lining (see pages 21–23).

2 Measure and cut lengths according to specific project. Cut two lengths for a self-lined swag; for a contrast swag, cut one length each of the face fabric and the contrast fabric.

3 Place fabrics right sides together. Measure in 15 inches from each end along one long edge; mark. Draw a line connecting each mark with corner on opposite edge, forming a taper. Cut along marked line through both layers.

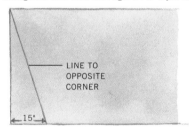

LINE TO OPPOSITE CORNER

15"

4 With pieces still right sides together, pin edges, leaving an 8-inch opening on one long edge. Stitch all around, making a $\frac{1}{2}$-inch seam. Clip points, press seams open. Turn swag right side out and press edges; slipstitch opening closed.

5 For attachment, see one of the following variations.

pouf swag

Rounded poufs accent this running treatment. You achieve the poufs, also called rosettes, by pulling a basic swag through harp-shaped, tulip-shaped, or circular swag holders.

The cut length equals $1\frac{1}{4}$ times the distance between the holders, plus 30 inches for each pouf, plus 2 times the cascade length, plus 1 inch.

POUF SWAG STEP-BY-STEP

1 Follow steps 1–5, "Running swags," this page, to make swag.

2 Mount swag holders according to manufacturer's instructions.

3 Lay swag flat on work surface, lining side up, and fold accordion style so short and long edges face in same direction. Folded swag should be about 4 inches wide.

SHORT EDGE   LONG EDGE

Using fabric scraps, tie swag loosely every 2 feet to keep folds in place.

4 From each end, measure finished length of cascade and slide rubber bands to this point. With short end facing center of window, drape swag over swag holders so rubber bands are behind holders. Remove ties.

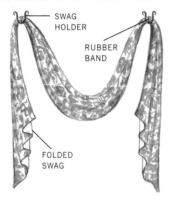

SWAG HOLDER

RUBBER BAND

FOLDED SWAG

5 From each holder, measure toward center 15 inches and mark with tape. Form a 30-inch loop so tape is at bottom of loop; place loop in holder. Remove rubber bands.

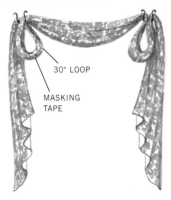

30" LOOP

MASKING TAPE

6 Adjust folds, pulling gently on the lower folds to lengthen the swag in the center and on the upper folds to keep top nearly straight.

7 To form each pouf, gently pull up the inner folds of the loop, fanning out the fabric as you pull.

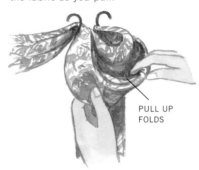

PULL UP FOLDS

Continue pulling out the folds until the pouf is full and rounded; tuck the top and bottom of the pouf back into the holder. Secure the pouf with pins. Adjust the folds in the swag and the cascades.

8 *For two swags* you will need three holders. Mark the midpoint of the swag. Measure and mark the cascades as for a single swag. Match the swag midpoint to the center holder. Measure 15 inches on each side of the midpoint for the center 30-inch loop; form the center pouf. Form the corner poufs the same way as you would for a single swag.

For three swags you will need four swag holders. Align the midpoint of the center swag with the center of the window.

scarf swag

Decorative rings and medallions are designed to hold graceful scarf swags. Ring-and-pole sets hold the swag in place by means of hook-and-loop fastener tape on the back of the pole; follow the manufacturer's instructions.

The cut length equals 1½ times the distance between holders or the pole length, plus 2 times cascade length, plus 1 inch.

SCARF SWAG STEP-BY-STEP

1 Follow steps 1–5, "Running swags," page 123, to make swag.

2 Mount swag holders according to manufacturer's instructions.

3 Follow step 3, "Pouf swag," this page, to fold swag. Or, for a softer look, gather swag in your hands.

4 Mark midpoints on swag and window. Lay swag over holders, lining up marks. Adjust folds, pulling gently on lower folds to lengthen swag at center and on upper folds to keep top nearly straight. Adjust cascades.

tab and knotted swags

Though they look very different, both tab and knotted swags are mounted on a board and held up at the corners in the same way.

With a tab swag, simple bands of fabric do the job; on a knotted swag, separate knots secure the swag and add visual interest.

For either style, the cut length equals the board size, plus 2 times the cascade length, plus 1 inch.

TABS. You can make self- or contrast-fabric tabs. Cut a strip of fabric 5 inches wide and 20 inches long. Fold strip lengthwise, right side in, and stitch long edges. Turn right side out, center seam at back, and press. Staple one end of the tab, seam up, to board 2 inches from the front and side.

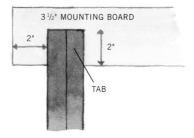

KNOTS. For a self-lined knot of medium-weight fabric, you need 1 yard for each knot; for sheer fabric, 48 inches. Fold fabric crosswise, right side in, and stitch cut edges together to form a tube (selvages will be at ends). For a contrast knot, you need 1/2 yard of each fabric. Stitch the two 18-inch pieces together, and then make the tube. Turn the tube right side out and tie a single knot slightly closer to one end than the other. With front end of knot down, staple long end of tube to board about 2 inches from front and side.

Starting at midpoint of covered board, staple swag to board. Gather swag in your hands, forming soft pleat. Pull tabs or knots up and over swag, angling end tabs or knots outward; staple and trim.

wrapped swag

This swag and cascade treatment "snakes" around the pole, forming two or more shallow swags with cascades. Single knots on either end secure the swag to the pole.

A wrapped swag can cover any window more that 36 inches wide. The cut length equals 1 1/2 times the pole size, plus 2 times cascade length, plus 1 inch, plus the knots (experiment to find length needed).

To make the swag, follow steps 1–5, "Running swags," page 123. Fold or gather the swag as in step 3, "Pouf swag," page 124.

Mark midpoints on swag and pole. Lining up marks, drape swag over pole at center, with half of swag in front and half behind. Tie a loose knot around the pole at each end. Adjust the folds in the swag, pulling gently on lower folds to lengthen it. Adjust the knots and cascades.

floral accents

Floral embellishments such as rosettes, choux, and cocards dress up a variety of window treatments. They can be used where swags meet, at the upper corners of cloud shades, or at the ends of tiebacks. Pin, stitch, or glue them in place.

ROSETTES

To make a rosette with a rounded appearance, you simply sew two ruffles out of contrast fabric and roll and stitch them together. For a plain, flat rosette, stitch swirls of gathered fabric to a circle of crinoline.

1 For a 6-inch, two-color rounded rosette, cut one 7-inch-wide strip from each of two fabrics. For a 4-inch flat rosette, cut one 3½-inch-wide strip and one 2-inch circle of crinoline. The cut length of each strip should be approximately 54 inches.

2 *Fold each strip in half lengthwise, wrong side in, and press. To gather, place one end of gimp cord or buttonhole twist ½ inch from lengthwise fold. Zigzag over cord, tapering for 6 inches until cord is ½ inch from lengthwise raw edges; continue zigzagging ½ inch from raw edge down length of strip.*

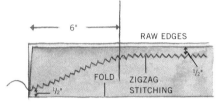

Trim excess fabric to ½ inch from stitching at tapered end. Gather strip to approximately 22 inches to make ruffle.

3 For a rounded rosette, *layer two ruffles so folded edge of bottom ruffle extends ¼ inch beyond edge of top ruffle. Starting at tapered ends, begin rolling ruffles tightly; using a long needle and a thimble, stitch through gathers at base as you go.*

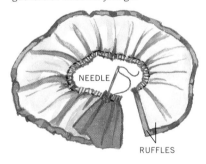

Continue rolling and stitching rosette, sewing through sides as rosette increases and folding under ends to conceal. If desired, cut and stitch a fabric circle to cover the raw edges at the center.

For a flat rosette, *position square end of ruffle on crinoline circle; tack.*

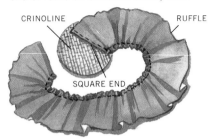

Stitch ruffle to edge of crinoline, letting folded edge overlap crinoline 1 inch. Continue stitching, working inward (ruffle will naturally coil). Push tapered end of ruffle into center; stitch to secure.

CHOUX

These decorative trimmings possess an old-fashioned charm. Choux can be made from the same or contrasting fabric; they are especially beautiful in soft silk. Start with an 11-inch square of fabric.

1 Fold the square of fabric in half diagonally, right side in. Hand-sew ½-inch-long running stitches along the edge of the fold, leaving a thread tail. Hand-sew ½-inch-long running stitches along one double-layer side of the triangle, close to the edge. Leave a tail at same point as previous stitching.

11" SQUARE OF FABRIC

2 Pin the point of the fabric with the thread tails to the center of a 6-inch square of crinoline. Pull both tails to gather the running stitches, and knot the thread tails together. Trim thread.

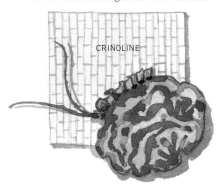

CRINOLINE

3 Turn the fabric right side out, and arrange the flower on the crinoline. Steam-press lightly to set folds. Lightly tack the fabric inside the folds to retain shape. Trim the extra crinoline.

COCARDS

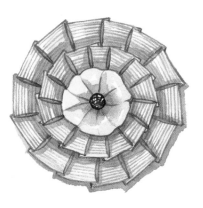

This tailored embellishment is borrowed from millinery and from military uniforms. Make it from 42-inch lengths of both 1-inch- and 1½-inch-wide grosgrain or other crisp ribbon on a 4-inch square of crinoline.

1 Cut the 1½-inch-wide ribbon into fourteen 3-inch pieces. Fold each piece in half, wrong side in, and string them with a hand needle onto knotted topstitching thread, piercing the unfolded corner ⅛ inch inside the top raw edges and right finished edge. Allow 1 inch of thread between the first strung piece and the last. Knot the thread after the last piece.

2 Join the knots at the beginning and end to form a circle. Trim thread.

3 Place the ribbon circle in the center of the crinoline. Flatten the ribbons and arrange the folded petals equidistant from one another. Pin each petal to the crinoline and hand-tack in place. Trim the crinoline.

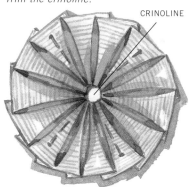

CRINOLINE

4 Repeat steps 1 and 2 using the 1-inch-wide ribbon. Pin this second ribbon circle on top of the first and hand-tack in place, as in step 3.

5 Embellish the center with a small gathered fabric ruffle similar to the rosette on page 126. Hand-tack in place, adding a decorative button for the flower center.

index